Beyond

Roger Cross is a senior fellow at the University of Melbourne whose nine books include *Fallout: Hedley Marston and the British bomb tests in Australia*. He is deeply interested in Australian history, science, and issues of social responsibility.

Avon Hudson is a long-time campaigner for a just solution to the human problems caused by the British atomic bomb tests in Australia. As an ex-serviceman himself, who served at Maralinga during some of the disastrous Minor Trials, he has intimate first-hand knowledge of the effects of radiation on human health.

BEYOND BELIEF

THE BRITISH BOMB TESTS:
AUSTRALIA'S VETERANS SPEAK OUT

ROGER CROSS
AND AVON HUDSON

Wakefield
Press

Wakefield Press
1 The Parade West
Kent Town
South Australia 5067
www.wakefieldpress.com.au

First published 2005

We have arranged for all royalties from the sale of this book to be
placed in a special account by our publisher in the hope to support
the erection of a suitable monument to all who worked under the
nuclear clouds.

Text designed by Clinton Ellicott, Wakefield Press
Typeset by Ryan Paine, Wakefield Press
Printed and bound by Hyde Park Press

National Library of Australia
Cataloguing-in-publication entry

Cross, R. T. (Roger T.).
Beyond belief: personal accounts from the atomic
bomb tests in Australia.

Bibliography.
ISBN 1 86254 660 6.

1. Radioactive fallout – South Australia – Maralinga.
2. Nuclear weapons – Testing – Personal narratives, Australian.
I. Hudson, Avon. II. Title.

363.1799/0994238

Publication of this book was assisted by the
Commonwealth Government through the
Australia Council, its arts funding and advisory body.

for all who felt the effects
of the unseen evil of ionising radiation

Contents

Preface: Setting the record straight

Beyond Belief is a collection of reminiscences by some of the people who got caught up in the British atomic bomb tests in Australia between 1952 and 1962. Our contributors include military personnel, civilian workers and Aboriginal people. Each of the personal histories has a thread in common, a link that binds them together: they are 'beyond belief'. They show how luck, or in these cases ill-luck, caused individuals and their families to be marked for life.

I met Avon Hudson at a public meeting in Adelaide, 2001, commemorating the dropping of the atomic bomb. As I listened to Avon's account I began to better understand the trauma that men and their families still suffered as a result of their involvement with the British bomb tests. It was clear that here was an important part of Australia's history that had been swept under the carpet for more than 40 years. I was deeply moved by what Avon had to say and after the meeting we determined to place on record – before it was too late – personal accounts of the experiences of some of the participants of the bomb tests.

This book is a monument, so take heed: be aware of your civic duty and demand a voice in the decisions that will affect you and future generations. Question the motives behind, and evidence for, any future involvement in weapons of mass destruction.

For and on behalf of all of the contributors
Roger Cross, 2005

1 – Setting the Scene

By the late 1940s the British government began to think about a test site for their first atomic bomb trial. They hoped to be able to use test sites in United States, but when the Americans proved difficult they decided to look elsewhere. On 16 September 1950 a top-secret personal message was sent from the British prime minister, Clement Atlee, to his Australian counterpart, Robert Menzies, requesting the use of Australia to explode British bombs. Menzies was flattered to be needed by the 'mother country'. Atlee's suggestion that the Monte Bello Islands be investigated as a possible site met with no difficulties. Menzies immediately agreed to the proposal – the Royal Commission into the tests held in 1984–1985 could find no evidence that he even consulted his cabinet colleagues – and the first atomic bomb exploded in Australia in 1952 was indeed in the remote Monte Bello Islands off the north-western coast of Western Australia.

In December 1952 Winston Churchill, now the British prime minister, asked Menzies for permission to test bombs at Emu Field in the far north of South Australia the following year, and once again permission was promptly granted. Two British bombs were 'tested' in October 1953 at Emu Field.

Britain did not explode atomic bombs in Australia again until 1956, during which year two tests took place on the Monte Bello Islands and four at Maralinga in South Australia's far west (with three more bombs to come in 1957 at Maralinga).

The power and the glory

The way in which the prime minister of Australia, Robert Menzies, came to give his permission for the British to explode atomic bombs on Australian soil involves his personal feelings towards the British as well as his perception of Australia's wider political aims. It concerns his subservience to Britain and the fear of Communism that was prevalent at the time. He wanted to lead Australia into the 'great game' of politics that instigated the atomic-bomb race. 'Between us', Howard Beale, Minister of Supply in the Menzies Government, is reported as saying, 'we shall build the defences of the free world and make historic advances in harnessing the forces of nature.' This statement alone reveals a great deal about how Australia was handed over to the ravages of the atomic-bomb explosions. It was all to do with political power and the optimism surrounding the advances of science – the power of the atom in the form of atomic bombs. However you care to explain the fact that Australia would let her territory be contaminated with radiation, it always comes back to weapons of mass destruction.

Always mindful of her sense of self-importance on the world stage, Britain was certainly not going to miss out on membership of the exclusive 'nuclear-bomb club'. Ernest Bevin, Foreign Secretary in the British Labour government of 1945–1951, is reported to have said as early as 1946: 'We have got to have this thing over here, whatever it costs. We have got to have a bloody Union Jack on top of it.' His government's decision was to involve thousands of Australians from all walks of life in what undoubtedly seemed at the time some great adventure.

These days the nuclear-bomb club is not so exclusive; many nations have the capacity to produce nuclear weapons. Membership of the club is well within the economic power of even small, non-national groups. Although the club is no longer exclusive in terms of technological expertise, it still has political and military value. There is no doubt that Australia has the know-how, and for a time we appear to have flirted with the idea of producing our own bomb. The technology and the materials for making nuclear weapons are in the hands of many, and nuclear war remains a continuing possibility.

In the 1950s, however, it was a very different affair. Ownership of such weapons was about exclusivity and being a top-ranking nation. Ownership would enable Britain to maintain her seat at the high table of nation states – regardless of her other attributes that made it seem rather a farce. Giving Britain the run of Australia to produce useable atomic bombs was to be our shield against the enemy, whoever that enemy was.

Gaining membership of the nuclear-bomb club during the first decade of scientific and technological nuclear knowledge was no easy matter. At the beginning it must have seemed that the sheer technical difficulties would ensure exclusivity – certainly the Americans hoped that such would be the case. But one of the major lessons we can learn from the history of the bomb is how difficult it is to prevent the spread of technology. Technological know-how spreads from the centre of knowledge and is soon found in the most unlikely places.

Like it or not, nuclear technology is used for peaceful purposes – developing radioactive materials for medicine and other industries, and for generating electricity. Australia's imported reactor at Lucas Heights (located in a closely settled part of Sydney) is a case in point. The decision to replace the ageing reactor at Lucas Heights with a new one seems to have been made on the basis of arguments by the nuclear lobby and scientists – that it would ensure the production of medical isotopes and enable research to continue. Those against, stated that medical isotopes can be produced in other ways. Perhaps the real reason for the huge capital expenditure can be found in a starkly simple explanation. Those who own a nuclear facility are able to swagger a little on the world's stage – it gives Australia a certain status, it always has.

The peaceful uses of nuclear energy can and have caused death and injury through the difficulty of containing the hazards of radiation from 'cradle to grave'. That is mining the ore, processing and refining, using in the nuclear facility and finally storage of the waste for thousands of years. The more complex the technology, the more likely it is that there will be a failure of one of the technological systems, or a human error leading to death and destruction. Only when the realisation came that any country able to operate a nuclear reactor had access to plutonium and was capable of producing nuclear weapons, were the seemingly clear-cut differences between the peaceful and military uses of nuclear weapons destroyed. Now if you have a nuclear power reactor, you are well on the way to making an atomic bomb.

In late-1940s Britain, the then Labour government felt (as it seems to today) that the country must continue to strut the world's stage. The bomb became a reality, a decision that was to have long-lasting implications for Australia. For the large number of individual men and their families who were caught up in the power games, the consequences have been life-changing. World War Two caused Australians to develop a greater self-reliance on home-grown industry – the atmosphere of the Cold War that followed World War Two provided a further stimulus. By the early 1950s, post-war reconstruction and optimism in Australia was expressed in the grandest of visions – the Snowy Mountains Scheme, another example of mastery over nature. The change from an agricultural to an industrial and technological society caught the imagination of the nation. And yet some things were too big to go it alone.

Backing a British bomb, with the aurora of protection and the political clout that came with it, was an enticing prospect. Aided and abetted by Australian physicists, the federal government saw the defence of Australia in terms of being a part of the nuclear-bomb club – if only as a provider of our wide open spaces. Vast tracts of the country were handed over for potential contamination by the British tests.

Indeed, the fact that the mother country needed Australia's help was flattering. Britain was still trusted to ensure that all would be well. When the British Atomic Weapons Research Establishment team (AWRE) set foot on Australian soil, they were welcomed by politicians and the Australian scientific community alike. The scientists embraced the opportunity provided by the British and their tests. Here was a chance for Australia to play a role in the 20th-century version of the Empire's 'great game' and demonstrate, perhaps for the first time in the history of Australian science, that they could be part of the action. Many of our nuclear scientists thought that the personal rewards would be great: they would gain influence and prestige. Their work might even be recognised enough for them to be elected to that most exclusive scientific club, The Royal Society of London. There was the possibility of political and social prizes too, that would enable the recipients to walk the corridors of power. Thoughts of personal aggrandisement such as awards in the Queen's honours lists, including knighthoods, were natural and in the case of Professors Ernest Titterton and Leslie Martin, they were not misplaced. Both were awarded knighthoods for the services they rendered to furthering the development of weapons of mass destruction.

The Cold War

After World War Two, rival super powers, the USSR and America, faced one another on the international stage, causing the conflict of the Cold War. The West saw this power struggle in cinematic terms as one between the 'good guys' and the 'bad guys'. So too did the Russians. In the early 1980s, the 'bad guys' were collectively known as the 'Evil Empire'. As in any B-grade movie, the 'good guys' are allowed a certain licence in pursuit of triumph over evil. Trespassing on the rights of individuals can be seen time and again throughout the accounts of the nuclear veterans.

The wonderfully popular and simplistic appeal of the forces of good over evil touched the subconsciousness of Judaeo-Christian peoples everywhere – Australians included. Here was a fight between Satan and God. A fight that would excuse any minor transgressions of human rights, whether putting servicemen at risk or taking away land from traditional Aboriginal owners.

The term 'guinea pig' arose in America as early as 1946, when certificates of membership to the Loyal Order of Guinea Pigs were circulated at Operation Crossroads. It is not surprising that Australian veterans have frequently used the term 'guinea pigs' to describe the way they were used.

Many nuclear veterans now worry about their grandchildren's health. However, this has been discounted as a mere neurosis by authorities like the Department of Veterans' Affairs (DVA). But recent evidence from a study by geneticists at the University of Leicester, Britain, suggests that far from such worry being a neurosis, they may have found a possible explanation for the leukaemia cluster around the British Sellafield Nuclear Plant, where childhood leukaemia is ten times the norm for Britain. It is possible, the researchers believe, for radiation-induced mutations to parts of the genetic code (DNA) to be passed on to later generations (*New Scientist*, 11 May, 2002, p. 5). Trying to waylay responsibility through such explanations as the neurosis theory is characteristic of the attitude encountered by successive governments of those nations involved with atomic testing. In a society where the scientific community was looked upon in awe by the general population, such explanations were readily accepted.

In what became known as 'nukespeak' during the Cold War, newspapers heralded the triumphant 'Mushroom Cloud' as a symbol of the defence of all that was good and righteous. Nukespeak does not tell of death and destruction, nor of the risk of cancers.

Secrecy over radiation sickness

After the Americans dropped atomic bombs on the Japanese cities of Hiroshima and Nagasaki in the culmination of World War Two, descriptions of the suffering of ordinary people were censored. The Australian journalist Wilfred Burchett managed to write first-hand about the 'atomic plague' (later called radiation sickness), which he witnessed on visiting Hiroshima only two weeks after the bomb was dropped on the city (on 6 August

1945), but further media reports were forbidden. The Japanese also suppressed references to the bombs – mention of the disaster was simply not allowed. Thus the world's public was denied the information that might have tempered enthusiasm for the bomb tests to come.

Les Dalton, in his book *Radiation Exposures*, states that 'a Japanese film, "The effects of the atomic bombs on Hiroshima and Nagasaki", showing the great human suffering in the wake of the blast, was confiscated. Not until 1968 was the film released publicly' (p. 102).

It took a while before it was realised that radioactivity was being spread around the world in an alarming manner by subsequent atmospheric tests. No one could escape, not even the most hawkish of the politicians and members of the military – their children were just as much at risk as anyone else's.

Both the people who died and those who survived the bombing of Japan are called the Hibakusha, which refers to the psychological effects they experienced. You can read more about this in Chapter 4 of this book.

Protests by 'Scientists for Peace'

In July 1957, a group of eminent scientists from the USSR, America, Poland, Japan, Britain, France, China, Canada, Austria and Australia met at the little town of Pugwash in Nova Scotia, Canada, to discuss the plight of the world. Our invited representative was Professor Mark Oliphant who, along with some of the most eminent scientists of the day, had heeded the appeal of Bertrand Russell and Albert Einstein to discuss increasing misgivings about nuclear weapons, war and weapons-testing. Their declaration illustrates that it was possible for sanity to prevail. They had significant impact on international politics and a limited test-ban treaty was signed by the nations involved. Their primary concern was the effect strontium-90, which was spreading around the world and increasing the incidence of leukaemia and bone cancer among the world's population.

The Pugwash Conference followed hard on the heels of

America's Professor Linus Pauling (one of the world's most important scientists), who demanded an A-Test Ban in the American press (Associated Press, 3 June 1957). Pauling, winner of the Nobel prize for chemistry in 1954, arranged for 2000 American scientists to sign his appeal. The appeal stated that 'each added amount of radiation causes damage to the health of human beings all over the world', and warned of 'an increase in the number of seriously defective children ... in future generations.' On 11 August 1958, the *New York Times* reported that the UN Scientific Committee on the Effects of Radiation were in agreement about the perils of radioactive fallout – even the smallest amounts of radiation were liable to cause mutations that would undermine heredity and inflict grave consequences upon the world's present and future population.

The Australian Atomic Weapons Tests Safety Committee

Something must be said about the body that was set up by the Australian government to safeguard its citizens from exposure to hazardous radiation from the bomb tests. Its members were to make assessments of the biological hazards of radioactive fallout over the country. The Safety Committee was constituted in July 1955, with Professor L H Martin (Defence Scientific Advisory) as chairman, Professor E W Titterton (head, School of Nuclear Physics, Australian National University), W A S Butement (chief scientist, Department of Supply), Dr C E Eddy (director, Commonwealth X-ray and Radium Laboratory), and Professor J P Baxter (Australian Atomic Energy Commission). The government meteorologist, Leonard Dwyer, was brought in a few weeks later.

So a committee of nuclear physicists – men who, to whatever extent, had a vested interest in the continuation of atomic bomb testing in Australia – was appointed by the Australian government to make judgements concerning the biological risks to humans and other forms of life.

The Safety Committee was reconstituted in March 1957, after Martin's resignation, with Titterton taking charge. While Martin and Titterton stand out as the pre-eminent members of the Safety Committee, Leonard Dwyer, the Commonwealth's Director of Meteorology, Department of the Interior, became a member of the Committee as an afterthought in 1955. After all, the Committee needed the best available advice about the weather conditions so that it would know when to allow the British to explode their bombs. The wrong wind direction could prove disastrous, especially if it meant that the radioactive cloud blew right over Maralinga Village.

Titterton had recently arrived from Britain where he had been working for the Atomic Energy Research Establishment at Harwell (AERE). Before that, he had worked in America on the Manhattan Project, developing the American atomic bombs. Titterton was assigned to the group dealing with the assembly and testing of nuclear weapons and, in the words of one author, pushed:

the first nuclear button, sending the signal that detonated the test weapon at Alamagordo, and when the shock wave from explosion reached him he said: 'It was wondrous'.

This seismic moment remained with Titterton throughout a lifelong advocacy of nuclear power and weapons. He returned to England in 1947, where he continued his defence physics work at the Atomic Energy Research Establishment, Harwell, until in 1951 Oliphant lured him to the Australian National University to become professor of nuclear physics. Titterton was involved in the British bomb project in Australia from its very beginnings in 1952, and was the one 'Australian' scientist the British trusted.

In 1956, Titterton published a book which listed six significant changes brought about by the atomic age – changes that he believed required Australians to 'adapt' the way in which they lived. The list had political, scientific and economic ramifications, all of which supported his underlying agenda: that the nuclear physicists' research and development efforts should be vigorously endorsed. As the new scientific elite, physicists were essential to Australia's advance into the future – not on the sheep's back, as formerly, but on the wing of the disintegrating atom. Their confidence at this time was supreme; as well as dominating scientific policy, they saw for themselves a role in regulating society itself.

Here was another opportunity to enhance physicists' influence with the government, a chance to push Australian science onto the international stage through significant participation in the testing programme. In the event, this did not occur: Britain still hoped for cooperation and the sharing of information with America, and while the use of Australia as a testing ground was one thing, Australian scientists as partners were a potential security liability the British could well do without.

There is no doubt about Titterton's agenda of self-promotion and the promotion of the nuclear option yet, viewed some 50 years on, his modus operandi often seems politically naive. Titterton was not held in high esteem by other scientists. Only weeks before testing was due to begin at Maralinga, he addressed South Australian concerns about what might lie ahead. In the following extract from an open letter written in terms of transparent simplicity to the people of South Australia, Titterton appealed to their patriotism (and played on their smouldering fear of Communism) as he explained why he and his colleagues were keen to be involved:

We are glad to have the opportunity of helping the Commonwealth defence effort in the development of weapons, which are a threat to no one but are intended as a deterrent to anyone who might wish to threaten others ... Apart from this we are very interested because A-weapons could be of vital importance in the defence of Australia itself ... [W]ith an air force equipped with tactical A-weapons, beach-heads could be smashed wherever they occurred ...'

There is a parallel to this kind of trickery in American history. In *American Ground Zero: The secret nuclear war*, Carole

Gallagher tells how the Mormons of Utah gradually became aware that their often fierce patriotism, and their religious beliefs, were rocked by the nuclear weapons tests in their State. They are known as the 'downwinders', and many have testified that the American Public Health Service officials stated that their neuroses about the fallout would make them sick, not the effects of radiation. Like these people, Australian and British servicemen trusted the authorities that were in place to protect them. They had faith in them, and now they suffer as a result.

Martin took a different approach than Titterton – 'hands-on' promotion of the nuclear option was quite alien to his nature. Where Titterton courted publicity and wooed the media, Martin shunned the limelight. In the first heady decade or so after the war, he was the key 'behind-the-scenes' man for government atomic energy research policy at the University of Melbourne.

Together with their personal ambitions, Martin and Titterton headed-up the management of the Safety Committee. Looking back, the task of the men who were to protect Australia from harm was undoubtedly difficult, if not impossible if they were expected to discharge their duties properly. Large areas of Australia were destined to receive some radioactive fallout from the explosions, and all that the Safety Committee could do was minimise the inevitable risks of damage to the health of the population.

The qualifications of the men making up the Safety Committee reflected the total ignorance of the Menzies Government in scientific matters. Not even a meteorologist was part of the panel as originally constituted. When it came to forming the Safety Committee, the government turned to Martin as its resident nuclear expert and first chairman. None of the members of the committee was a biologist. Thus nuclear physicists came to be responsible for a nation's safety, responsible for judgements concerning the biological risks to human and other forms of life. Half a century later, this seems more than a little strange. We should remember, however, the prevailing power structure within Australian science: the physicists were in complete ascendancy, and the atomic question was their 'baby'. Never mind that in matters of safety they were not competent to judge. Their political influence was such that the Australian government appointed them unquestioningly to the Safety Committee, and once there relied on them to make assessments on its behalf. That they could not do so was hardly their fault, and the blame has to lie elsewhere – it was not as if the experts were unavailable, after all.

The Australian government must stand condemned for a crucial error of judgement. But then, the committee's chairman, Martin, did not seem to know what was needed, either. We will never know if things would have been better if the Safety Committee had a competent biochemist as a member.

All this aside, the Safety Committee did not have jurisdiction over the Maralinga or the Monte Bello Islands sites where atomic bombs were detonated after the formation of the committee in 1955. That fell to the Range Commander, who was nominally an Australian, but in reality the British made all the decisions.

The relationship between the Australian Range Commander and the British needs further study. Our conversations with Australian servicemen point to the British Bomb Group making all the significant decisions and the Range Commander looking after day-to-day running of the facilities – especially the Maralinga Village. He was charged with the responsibility of enforcing safety regulations and he was responsible for 'bringing the Safety Regulations and all other relevant Health Physics safety regulations to the knowledge of all staff and visitors at the Range'. This was rarely done, as the testimony of the veterans proves.

The bomb was exploded on 2 October:
25 kilotons fired at 8 am

The Monte Bello Islands are a group of little-known, uninhabited islands off the north-west coast of Western Australia. They lie roughly north of the town of Onslow, approximately 90 kilometres from the coast at its closest point. To say that they are lonely is stating the obvious. They are rocky outcrops made up of coral and limestone with a highest point of only about 38 metres above sea level. The islands were named in 1801–1802 by the French navigator Nicolas Baudin, commander of the French exploration fleet in Australian waters, in honour of Marshal Lannes, whom Napoleon created Duke of Montebello. In the early seventeenth century, the English ship the *Tryal* was wrecked on what subsequently became known as Tryal Rock. Two boatloads of survivors made it to what was then Batavia, with the Dutch East India Company subsequently marking Tryal Rock on its charts.

The choice to carry out testing on these islands, according to the 1984 Royal Commission, was made on the basis that Britain had many ports used for international shipping. What if there was an attack on British harbours and an atomic bomb explosion occurred below the waterline, perhaps in the hold of a ship? An assessment of what would happen was needed. In 1950, British prime minister, Clement Attlee, asked Robert Menzies for permission to survey the islands and naturally this was given.

The Monte Bello Islands and the sites of
all three tests held there

The first atomic bomb test was conducted as a military operation. A special task force was assembled under the command of Rear Admiral Torlesse with five ships, including HMS *Plym* in which the bomb was to be planted. The British were well aware of the adverse meteorological conditions in that part of Australia, and the likelihood that radiation from the test would be carried east over the Australian mainland, then on to countries as far away as Fiji and possibly New Zealand. The Royal Commission states: 'The Monte Bello Islands were not an appropriate place for atomic tests owing to the prevailing weather patterns and the limited opportunities for firing.' In fact, October was the only month in the year when there was a chance that the wind might not blow towards the mainland.

Standby for Britain's first atomic bomb test began on 1 October 1952, but the wind conditions were not favourable that day. The weapon was fired at 8 am local time the following day. The yield was about 25 kilotons, but this says nothing about the amount of radioactivity released. Some bombs are 'dirty' and produce excessive amounts of radioactive debris, while others release far less. The cloud rose into a complicated wind pattern, which varied with height. Aircraft sorties were made to try and ascertain what happened to the radioactive cloud. The prevailing winds sent the cloud over the mainland and its low height meant that any rain would cause significant 'rainouts' of radioactivity (the radioactivity is literally washed to earth by rain). Fallout was reported in some places across the country at 200 times the normal background level, while three of the five Lincoln bombers flying out of Townsville, Queensland, recorded significant radioactivity on a section between Townsville and Rockhampton. The successful test meant that Britain became the third power after America and the USSR to explode an atomic bomb.

Before his death in April 2002, Ian McKiggan collected reminiscences from people who were associated with the tests. Mr Dennis Cole was the manager of the Commonwealth Hostel at Exmouth – the nearest town to American/Australian Radio Communications Base at the North West Cape. He was at Onslow during the 1952 Monte Bello bomb test. Lieutenant Commander Jerry Lattin recounts a practical joke that beggars belief. Dick Sundstrom of Traralgon, Victoria, was on HMAS *Sydney* as a member of the ship's company. He was a naval airman, in the armaments section. He witnessed the first British atomic bomb explosion. Bob Dennis is one of the few people alive who was on duty for the Australian navy at all three Monte Bello atomic bomb tests.

Dennis Cole

The British Bomb Group constructed a bomb assembly area outside Onslow. To transport the assembled bomb to the 'host' ship HMS *Plym* (the bomb was set off in the *Plym* and blew it to smithereens), they had commandeered a Western Australian Government Railways (WAGR) locomotive and some rolling stock. The railway line ran down the centre of the street and out onto the long Onslow jetty. When all was ready, in accordance with a strictly specified timetable, the infernal device was loaded into a boxcar and the 'choo-choo' set off into town and down the main street escorted by a detachment of British Royal Marines. At noon the train came to an abrupt and unscheduled halt. The driver, a veteran WAGR man, climbed down from his platform and started across the road to the adjacent Onslow pub.

'Where the hell are you going?' shrieked the Chief Pom.

'To have me lunch.'

'You've got to be joking! Get that train moving!'

'Nope. Union rules. Twelve to one. Lunch.'

And lunch he had. About a dozen beers, while the Brits kept a panicky eye on their precious cargo. That was the last time they let an Australian get anywhere near one of their bombs!

Lieutenant Commander Jerry Lattin by Ian McKiggan

Jerry asked me if I remembered HMAS *Warrego*. I said yes, of course, she was a sloop, and a sister ship to HMAS *Swan*. The *Warrego* had been built before World War Two and by the 1950s she had become a survey ship—she was painted white. She made a special radiation survey of the Monte Bellos in October and November 1955, six months prior to the Mosaic tests.

'Right,' said Jerry. 'Well, many years later, when Joe Doyle was serving on the *Warrego*, they had an Admiral's Inspection. You remember what's involved in Admirals' Inspections?'

I did. The bastards want to see everything.

'Right again,' said Jerry. 'This time the Admiral was about to leave when he suddenly asks to see the ship's radiation monitoring equipment.' These are standard issue for all Naval ships.

'Well they lay the monitors out on the quarter-deck and the Admiral ordered them to be switched on. And when they did, every bloody needle went hard a' starboard. All the counters started squawking. Of course at first they thought that the machines were faulty. They checked 'em out and they were in working order. Panic. Was the whole ship radioactive? No. Eventually they traced the radiation to one powerful source right down near the keel in the tiller flat. Some malevolent bastard had cemented it in, years before.'

I was stupefied. How could anyone be so moronic? For at least fifteen years many sailors would have been living literally right on top of that uninvited guest.

I had lunch with Joe Doyle at the Sydney Rugby Club a few weeks later, and cross examined him. He swears it's true. I still can't get over it – how many people are going to die because of it?'

Dick Sundstrom

It happened at 8 am on 3 October 1952. We had departed Sydney for a 'mystery' cruise on 30 August 1952, eventually arriving in the Monte Bellos on 27 September. We were dressed in sandals, shorts and tee-shirts. The *Sydney* had a crew of around 1300 and hundreds of us witnessed the explosion from the flight deck. I stood with two of my mates, Geoff Baker and Clyde Player. The radioactive cloud came right over us – we watched it for about one and a half hours. [On the day of the test the HMAS *Sydney* was on patrol with HMAS *Macquarie* in the Indian Ocean at a distance of around 100 miles from the site of the explosion.]

We were totally unaware that there was any danger from radioactive fallout. Clyde Player ate an apple while the cloud passed overhead. Clyde was a fitness fanatic; he spent a lot of time in the gym. It is not funny that this fit man should die of stomach cancer about six years later. The authorities said, 'he probably strained his muscles lifting weights'. I ask you, would you die of stomach cancer doing that? I have often wondered about eating that apple!

Geoff Baker died from liver cancer about ten years later. I have had 170 skin cancers removed and a low-grade B-Cell lymphoma removed in July 2001 and another in December 2002. A recent MRI scan at the Monash Medical Centre in Melbourne shows extensive lymph problems at the back of my throat. I am sorry to say that my daughter was born with a hole in her back; nobody knew what caused it – I have often wondered about the connection between this and my exposure to radiation.

I think HMAS *Sydney* has had about a 70-per-cent death rate

HMAS Sydney

from that test. The *Sydney* used to desalinate the sea water and I have often wondered whether we were drinking water contaminated by radioactivity. The clothes we wore when we witnessed the explosion were not thrown out, we just carried on as usual. The day after the test (3 October) we sailed to Shark Bay for eight to nine days, I think we may have followed the radioactive cloud down the coast.

If you ask me how the experience has affected me over the years, I can say it has in three ways. First, it has affected my own health. Secondly, there are the continuing memories and knowledge of the damage that has been done by nuclear radiation. If only we had been treated better by the authorities saying: Look you have all been exposed to high levels of radioactivity, let's see if we can make things easier for you and your families. But no one believes us. Thirdly, my daughter's health problems. Fortunately a specialist gave her treatment that worked.

———

We must ask the question: What was the motive behind ordering HMAS *Sydney* and its crew to come in close enough to the explosion for there to be a risk of contamination? The navy high command would want its seamen to carry on regardless of atomic bombs exploding in their vicinity. Might the thinking have been to expose the crew to a simulated theatre of war? At the time it must have seemed like a wonderful opportunity to see whether a ship's crew would keep its nerve and maintain discipline. The *Sydney*'s crew was deliberately exposed to an extreme hazard for the purpose of future operational planning. The crew was experimented upon; their health, and possibly the health of their children, was to be risked for information about the nature of carrying out operations in a radioactive area. The military authorities of the 'nuclear powers' routinely tested their servicemen for their 'physical and psychological endurance on simulated radioactive battlefields' (Dalton 1991, p. 106). Other explanations as to the motive of the naval authorities are possible, some more generous than others, but none are as convincing. For example, a shipping-exclusion zone was declared around the islands to protect friendly vessels from radiation hazards and to warn-off enemy spy ships. The *Sydney* was probably part of the operation to enforce this exclusion zone.

Of course, for the sailors it was seen as a bit of light relief from the tedium of patrolling the waters around the lonely and remote Monte Bellos. It was, at least, a chance to witness one of the 20th century's grand events and, incidentally, the power and might of Britain. But that is being generous.

Bob Dennis

In 1952 I had my first introduction into atomic testing. I was a national service man on HMAS *Culgoa*–being an ordinary seaman. We were up at the Monte Bello Islands under the impression that we were just patrolling the area, keeping a look out for any Russian submarines that might come up or any other intruders, to keep them out. [Actually, HMAS *Culgoa* also acted as a weathership for the test.] To this day I am not certain how far away we were from the explosion. [They were stationed about 300 miles south-west of

Monte Bello.] We were advised, when the explosion took place, to face a southerly direction so obviously we were steaming away from the explosion when it happened. We saw a cloud in the distance but I don't know whether it was a radiation cloud. Being ordinary seamen we weren't told much about it and we didn't think it was anything of great importance to us. It was, I suppose, a bit of a novelty at the time – the family called me Monte Bello Bob for a while! Very few people had been to the Monte Bello Islands and most people didn't even know where they were. For an 18 year old it was just one of life's experiences – a bit of notoriety at the time.

––––––––

Following the explosion, some of the ships re-entered the immediate vicinity of the bomb site to recover scientific instruments. This work was done by the British (the Royal Commission notes that only one Australian was involved). The sea water received a great deal of radioactivity and was badly contaminated. This radioactive contamination was undoubtedly fed into the human food chain through the desalination of water for human consumption. The Royal Commission states that distillation of the sea water was stopped when the dose rate reached a low level that had nothing to do with a safe limit, but rather to do with the limit of the sensitivity of the measuring instruments. To what extent Australian ships distilled contaminated water is not known.

Another of the HMAS ships was seriously contaminated. This was the *Koala*, which had been detailed to recover a sunken landing craft near Daisy Island. This was done but the landing craft was heavily contaminated with radioactive sand and mud. This craft was dumped in deep water but not before *Koala* was also contaminated. The crew had walked in the mud and sand and spread it about the ship; even the captain's carpet was contaminated. Decontamination took two days. The Royal Commission notes that the divers who went down to attach cables to the landing craft were exposed to the risk of ingesting radioactive sea water.

There were two other groups who received doses of radiation. One case involves the Joint Services Training Group, who worked out of HMAS *Hawkesbury*, which sailed for the Monte Bello Islands from Fremantle on 27 October 1952. A camp was set up on South East Island where the group undertook a number of training exercises to give the men practical experience in re-entry and recovery work and decontamination procedures, as well as to produce a radiation contamination survey for Trimouille Island. These men were deliberately ordered into a highly contaminated area.

The other case, involving the poorly planned programme of air sampling undertaken by the RAAF, was more serious. The Royal Commission was highly critical of this programme, for it seems that no orders were issued as to the radiological safety of the flight or ground crews. The aircrew did not carry dosimeters, and the Lincoln bombers that were used had no gamma-ray detection equipment installed. The Wing Dakotas also carried out operations and on 4 October they encountered intense radioactivity with the measuring equipment on board showing that the aircraft were contaminated. The Royal Commission states that the categorical assurance by the British that there was no risk to aircrews was false – crews did receive significant doses of radiation. Just how much we will never know.

It must be remembered that the first atomic bomb test occurred over 50 years ago, and the number of men who still survive their experiences is quite small. Also, Australia's main involvement was to provide naval support for this 'military' operation. They were not meant to be there. They had no control over the directives that were put in place by the military personnel. They were taken advantage of. And the 1952 bomb was just a foretaste of what was to come.

The bombs were exploded on 15 October: 10 kilotons fired at
7 am; 27 October: 8 kilotons fired at 7 am

These two bombs were exploded at the disastrous Emu Field
site in the far north of South Australia (200 miles north of
Maralinga and 300 miles from Woomera, the rocket range set
up by the British in 1946). Len Beadell, whose exploits in the
back country of Australia are well-known (he blazed the first
east–west road across the centre of Australia), surveyed the area
and wrote about his experiences in his book *Blast the Bush*.
In this book he suggests that the British had no idea of the
remoteness of Emu. Len Beadell was told to find a site well
away from Woomera, presumably because the radiation would
be too dangerous for their huge investment in rocket work
there. Certainly, after the two Totem bombs were exploded
there in 1953, the British couldn't get away quick enough – the
site was not used again.

The Emu Field site, a claypan called Dingo in the South
Australian desert, was almost immediately found to be a terrible
choice. It is desert country with no water, and the sand in
the surrounding hills is soft and yielding. Heavy machinery
became bogged in the sand, it was difficult to keep the site
supplied, and the sand storms played havoc with sensitive
equipment.

Although the chosen site was extremely isolated from
main centres of population, many people were affected by
the tests carried out there. Only passing thought was given to

the possibility of nomadic or semi-nomadic Aborigines using the area. This was, after all, an area of Australia that was little-known at the time and few people were aware of the presence of Aboriginal people.

The Aborigines in the area were largely or wholly unclothed and the status of their general health was unknown. There were few methods of communicating the dangers to them. They cooked in the open and ate traditional foods that collected radioactivity from the tests. (When an animal eats contaminated food, biological magnification occurs, which concentrates the radiation that was then absorbed by the Aborigines.)

By 1953, traditional patterns of Aboriginal movement had broken down due to the establishment of Christian missions. The Pitjantjatjara people of the north moved further south to the transcontinental railway line, where they set up camp at the Ooldea mission. Others had moved to various missions and pastoral stations, the attraction of European food being a powerful incentive. But according to the Royal Commission, the area was still being used for occasional visits – for 'hunting and gathering, for temporary settlements, for caretakership and spiritual renewal ... From an unknown time – but certainly for long before the arrival of white people – Aboriginal people had used the lands where the tests took place ... people were constantly traversing the country'. In contrast, William Penney (later Sir William), Chief of the British Atomic Weapons Group, asked W A S Butement, Australia's chief scientist with the Department of Supply, about indigenous Australians. He was told that: 'I am given to understand that the area is no longer used for Aborigines ... there is no need whatever for Aborigines to use any part of this country around the proposed area' (Milliken 1986, p. 165).

Walter MacDougall was involved in the Emu Field tests. He became a native patrol officer in 1947 and was attached to the Woomera Rocket Range. He was responsible for an increasingly large area of patrol. He struggled to make sure that the Aborigines in the area were not affected by the Woomera rocket tests but, as his work increased, so too did the problems of maintaining contact with the tribal people. By 1950 he had become concerned that there was not a census of the people living in this vast area, whose range stretched 1200 miles across South Australia's far north to the Western Australian coast.

In August 1951, MacDougall came across some tribal Aborigines who had been avoiding contact with whites. He gradually extended his patrols during 1952, into some of the most difficult country imaginable, finding yet more groups avoiding the white missions in the northern boundaries of the Central Reserve. In April 1953, MacDougall searched the area around the Emu site called Granite Downs, and was able to map traditional territory of the Yankunytjatjara people. Many uncertainties still remained, such as the water sources used by the Aboriginal people.

The minutes of the Totem Panel's fourth meeting (2 April 1953) illustrate the level of concern over the Aboriginal problem. First in order of presentation came the petty thefts by Aboriginals from the Totem site. In second place only came concern over the danger of them entering the contaminated area at the actual test site. It was decided to undertake aerial patrols of the test area – at most covering a 20-mile range – and warnings of the coming trials were sent to pastoral station managers in August 1953.

The Yankunytjatjara people at Wallatinna Station, a pastoral property on Granite Downs, only 108 miles from the Totem 1 site (a ten kiloton bomb) were seriously contaminated and suffered radiation sickness after what became known as the infamous 'Black Mist Incident' recorded in the Royal Commission's report. The secretary of the Pitjantjatjara Council, Robert Stevens, claimed in a report that a black mist had rolled across the outback in 1953, affecting a large number of the Aboriginal people and some European Australians whom subsequently died. About 45 Yankunytjatjara Aboriginals were enveloped in a black mist one or two days after the explosion. One of the Aboriginal women, Jessie Lennon, tells how the mist (smoke) came, 'it filled up the hills, the holes, rolled in along the ground and as high as the tree tops.' Andrew Collet (lawyer for the Maralinga Tjarutja people) says that only the station owners and Walter McDougall knew what happened. Jessie Lennon noticed the mist smelled like metal – like Port Pirie (the South Australian town famous for its smelting of the Broken Hill ore) smells. The following accounts are from Aboriginal people and European civilian and military personnel who were enveloped in the Black Mist.

Eileen Kampakuta Brown

It [the black mist] came when the sun was going down ... We thought the farmers were burning stumps ... We thought we were close [to the fire] that is why the smoke [fallout] caught us. We got up in the morning from our tents ... everyone had red eyes. ... We tried to open our eyes in the morning but we couldn't open them. We had red eyes and tongues and our coughing was getting worse. We were wondering what sort of sickness we had. There was no doctor only the two station bosses. All day we sat in our tents with our eyes closed. Our eyes were sore, red and shut. We couldn't open them. We were coughing ... All people got sick right up to Oodnadatta and all the way over that way.

Within 48 hours, many were suffering from rashes, vomiting, headaches, peeling skin and diarrhoea – all typical signs of radiation sickness (see the chapter 'Radiation: Its nature and the hazards'). After about 72 hours, many of the children became temporarily blind and within a few days the old and the frail were dying. Following the incident, nearly 20 people were buried on the outskirts of Wallatinna Station. Many more died over the next 12 months but the numbers are unknown.

Three more Aboriginal women corroborate Eileen's story. Millie Taylor reports that her mum developed a large lump in her throat, while Jessie Williams' mother became very sick. Edna Williams tells how it was a hot calm day and 'we could see the smoke coming down. All the kids were sick then. Dark sort of smoke – funny smell.' Jessie Williams says that even though they were hungry they couldn't eat – 'we felt very sick and everything tasted funny.'

The Adelaide *Advertiser* reported a claim from a Dr Trevor Cutter, member of the Central Australian Aboriginal Congress working for an Alice Springs health service, suggesting that there had been between 30 and 50 Aboriginal fatalities among up to 1000 affected people. He stated that Aboriginal people who had been in five different locations (Coffin Hill, Ernabella, Kenmore Park, Everard Park and Granite Downs) recalled the terror of the Black Mist. (We have attempted to obtain the correspondence between Cutter and the relevant departments of the South Australian government, through its *Freedom of Information Act*. Disclosure was refused on the grounds that it is covered by the secrecy provisions of the *State Radiation and Protection and Control Act*, 1982.) When this incident first came to light in 1980, Titterton, former chairman of the Safety Committee, said on an ABC programme:

No such thing can possibly occur. I don't know of any black mists. No black mists have ever been reported until this scare campaign was started ... [I]f you investigate black mist sure you're going to get into an area where mystique is the central feature.

Despite Titterton's remarks, an inquiry was initiated by the Federal Minister for Science and the Environment on 18 September 1980, and was carried out by the Australian Ionising Radiation Advisory Council (AIRAC). Its report lends credibility to the incident: 'It is evident that the passage of the cloud over or near Wallatinna would have been visible for a considerable distance to either side of its path' (AIRAC 1983, p. 49).

There the matter rested until 1982 when an Aboriginal man of the Yankunytjatjara people, Yami Lester, heard a radio interview with Titterton, who gave the categorical assurance that no Aboriginal people had been harmed by any of the tests. Lester had been working as a boy on Wallatinna Station at the time of the Totem tests. He heard Titterton say, in answer to a question about the care of Aboriginal people: 'Oh, the black people were well looked after . . .' Yami said to himself 'bullshit, he is talking the wrong way.' He was so angry that he rang the *Advertiser* in Adelaide and the paper then ran a series of reports on the tests.

The 1984 Royal Commission visited Wallatinna Station and heard evidence from a number of the Yankunytjatjara tribe who were camped in the area at the time. Yami Lester spoke of his own experience:

I heard a big bang – a noise like an explosion and later something come in the air '. . . [it] was coming from the south, black-like smoke. I was thinking it might be a dust storm, but it was quiet, just moving . . . through the trees and above that again, you know. It was just rolling and moving quietly (Royal Commission 1985, pp. 174–175).

Yami Lester reports that an uncle of his, Harry, and the white owners of Wallatinna Station, also saw and experienced the cloud (Lester 2000). Lester recounts how the old people were frightened, thinking that it was a spirit, and how they tried to direct it away from their camp with woomeras (implements used to propel spears at distant objects with great force). Others told of how the cloud was low to the ground; it was, they said, like a black mist rolling over the scrub. Afterwards the water tasted sweet.

Almerta Lander reported seeing the cloud passing through Wallatinna – a cloud that rolled along dropping a fine, sticky dust as it went. Mr Ernest Giles at Welbourne Hill Station also heard the explosion, and saw a 'mountain of smoke in the distance'.

The Black Mist Incident was certainly real and radioactive contamination did cause illness. Mr David Barnes, the British health physicist responsible for safety at the Totem tests, stated under cross examination by the Royal Commission that '[W]e might have taken more account of the Aboriginal population', and that Totem 1 was designed to be five kilotons but was in fact ten kilotons. The fallout over Aboriginal hunting grounds had been 100 per cent above the recommended safe level.

Almerta Lander's experiences of the Black Mist support all the other reports. She has contributed a poem, which is included after her story.

Almerta Lander

At the time of the atomic bomb tests at Emu Plains, my husband, James (Mack) Lander was a contractor building yards for Mr Phil Giles of Welbourne Hill Station. We camped at a bore known as 'Never Never'. Three of our children were there. Jim was at school at Alice Springs.

At the time we had a small caravan but we slept outdoors. As it was impossible to cook in the caravan – on account of the heat – I cooked all our meals in camp ovens. We boiled salt meat in buckets on the open fire and boiled our billy tea there too. You can see we led a very outdoor life.

We had previously lived at a place called Dallarinna, which is now part of Wallatinna Station, about 175 kilometres from Emu. I mention this because of its proximity to 'Never Never' Station. Many Aboriginal people lived at Mintabie and many died after the 'black cloud' passed over them.

At no time did anyone officially tell us that the trials were about to begin. Vague rumours had been circulating which we dismissed as just that.

The day of the Emu bomb test: The lead up

On the day of the atomic bomb trial, our day began as any other. The children played around the caravan, the dogs eyeing them lazily, they – the dogs and children – began chasing lizards and were now tired of that game. I carried all the salt meat out to cook in the bucket of boiling water on the open fire and I checked on the bread baking in the camp oven. Calling the children to me, we then set out on our daily walk to the yard, carrying with us a billy of tea for 'smoko'.

As we walked, I noticed how silent it was (remember the explosion occurred at 7 am). Usually there were many crows around cawing raucously. Other birds kept us company too: butcher birds, cockatoos and little finches. This day, except for some kites coasting around high in the sky, there were none. Why? It puzzled me but I did not dwell on it. We sat in the sparse shade of a Mulga tree drinking our tea and talking. Mack decided that he would walk back with us to refill his water bag. As we walked, he too, was struck by the silence and absence of birds and remarked upon it. The children were quiet after their walk and the dogs padded silently behind them.

In the sky an unusual cloud appeared. It was like a broad ribbon. It stretched across the sky at a low altitude. As we watched, it moved further across the sky, travelling from west to east, and finger-like clouds dangled from its fringe. Later, an official observer sent out in a plane to track its direction confirmed this description.

The day of the cloud

The children accompanied their father to the door of the caravan while I checked on the bread in the camp oven. Finding it cooked, I was about to take it out when I heard Mack shout 'Dust Storm!' There had been no dusty wind blowing but dust storms can arise very quickly and can be quite violent and destructive, taking any loose articles in their path. I didn't want to be hurt by a flying object or be smothered in dust, so I left the bread and ran to the caravan. As we watched its progress through the window, we saw that it was no ordinary dust storm. A black cloud was slowly and quietly rolling through the scrub. To us it was quite sinister because of its blackness and because it seemed to be creeping upon us. It was definitely not a dust storm.

We watched in fascination as it drew nearer. Our doors and windows were shut and it was rather stifling but it became much worse when the dust began sifting through the cracks—a fine grey dust which made us cough and sneeze and our eyes water. It grew dark as it rolled over and disappeared in the distance. We ventured out cautiously and saw that grey dust lay over everything. We dusted our clothes off the best we could and washed our faces and hands, and then we tackled the dust inside the caravan. It was so fine and silky; it seemed to dance away from our dusters, then settle back in the same spot. It was impossible to shift it. We were eventually obliged to wash it off using some of our precious water, which we carted from the bore and kept covered in 44-gallon drums.

Outside, the salt meat in the bucket was inedible as it was covered in grey scum. The camp-oven lid had protected the bread. We dusted it off and ate it. I walked around the fireplace and each step I took, a puff of grey dust arose around my bare legs, some settling on my face and neck. It was everywhere, so sticky and pervasive.

Mack returned to his yard building and the children were once more chasing lizards. They coughed and sneezed as they ran. The strange cloud had disappeared except for the dust, our lives were normal again.

After the Black Cloud

No one ever came to advise us that the 'dust' was the fallout from the bomb. It was as though we didn't exist. Maybe to them we didn't as we were just a handful of people in an isolated place in the bush. Rumours were again rife and this time we were very much inclined to believe them. Newspapers began speculating that something had gone horribly wrong. (We know that the bomb was about twice the intensity as that predicted.) Perhaps a sudden wind change or there was a miscalculation of the direction causing the dust to blow into inhabited regions. There were accusations and denials: neither the British government, who were conducting the trials, nor the Australian government who had permitted them, wished to take the blame.

Shortly after, word went around that a sickness was laying low the Aboriginal people living at Wallatinna and Mintabie. Old people and young children were dying, their bodies covered in sores and their eyes weeping. No medical specialists visited them or any doctor as far as I can remember and it was assumed that it was a measles epidemic. Who really knows what caused the sickness? Was it more convenient not to know? Surely a radiation test was not beyond the realms of possibility. It seems very coincidental that it occurred after the black cloud had covered them in its filthy dust. We did not have sickness ourselves but Aboriginal immune systems are not as effective as ours.

However, my son John, now in his fifties, suffers from a lung complaint – as yet undiagnosed. He has had numerous tests done by specialists at the Royal Adelaide Hospital and here in Alice Springs he has seen a visiting specialist on numerous occasions. As for myself, I have had very bad skin problems – mainly scaly patches on my legs and face. I have had a malignant melanoma removed from my neck and other small cancers removed surgically with grafts to follow. At no time has anyone ever suggested any further tests. Indeed, there seems to be an air of disbelief whenever I explained that I had been exposed to dust from atomic trials.

My daughter, Rosemary, was a student at a high school in Alice Springs, when a teacher was lecturing on atomic bombs. Rosemary raised her hand and remarked that she had seen an atomic bomb, which of course she had. A few years [after the 1953 incident] we had all seen the mushroom cloud of the Maralinga tests quite plainly. She was sharply told to put her hand down and not be stupid, much to the amusement of the class and my daughter's humiliation. I tell this story to show the general ignorance, even among educated and intelligent people, of the fact that atomic tests had been performed in Australia.

The Royal Commission

The years went by and we moved around working on various stations in South Australia, chiefly in the northern parts. My husband died and the children (now teenagers) and I moved to Alice Springs.

By this time, the Australian air force men and soldiers, who believed they had been used as guinea pigs at the tests, were demanding answers. At last an enquiry was commissioned, headed by Justice Jim McClelland in conjunction with a team of barristers representing the Australian and British governments and for the Aboriginal people. [A meeting of] the Commission was held at Marla, a small town south of Alice Springs and close to Wallatinna Station where many Aboriginal people who had survived the sickness still lived.

Quite unexpectedly, I was asked if I would appear as a witness. At first I refused as I am a rather retiring sort of person. One day I heard on the radio a discussion about the black cloud and an English officer was quoted as remarking, 'Tell the people of Oodnadatta it was a dust storm. They wouldn't know the difference.' This remark convinced me that I should show them that we did know the difference. That is how I came to give evidence at the enquiry. I was the only European witness at Marla.

Many questions and answers were given, but in the end I don't think much was achieved. The two governments made a few token gestures but many important issues were never answered, nor are they to this day.

No one has ever contacted us, but no one could overlook the fact that defence personnel were deployed in the experiments: air force men and soldiers who were right at the 'coal face' as they are today. Surely they should be given the same recognition as forces in combat zones at war. After all, they were exposed to equally great danger.

The Black Cloud

In the morning, early were three loud bangs,
Wannambi, the water snake, will soon show his fangs,
Cried old Yakety, in great delight,
'There will be plenty of rain falling tonight.'

In all the great sky there was not even a cloud,
But we were too scared to tell him out loud.
'Then It came,' the young man said, 'in the full light of day,
A great, black cloud, covering all in its way.'

Alarmed, we watched it draw near, and ever near,
Our voices raised in a loud cry of fear.
There was no wind, the birds had ceased their cries,
Thick darkness came, blotting out the skies.

Terrified we stood, not knowing where to go,
The old women wailed, and bent down low,
Gathering us children into their skinny arms
To protect us from this spirit's evil charms.

Strong men, and feeble men, all began to dig
Wildly in the creek bed, making a hole so big
To cover us all, the little ones, but not me,
I was too big, besides, I wanted to see.

Like bush-fire smoke, the cloud covered us all,
An evil presence. Then we began to call
One to another, with trembling, husky words,
'What is it? Where are the animals? Where are the birds?'

No birds sang, no creatures moved in the land,
We walked away slowly, holding by the hand
The small children. All of us scared, but seemingly well,
Though my eyes were stinging, and some of us fell.

Days after, the terrible sickness came. The babies were the worst
Their bodies smothered in awful sores, to die they were the first.
Our skin peeled off in strips and our eyes were sore.
Weakening, we called on our ancient healing lore,

None came to help us and so we died,
Laying the bodies in the sand, side by side.
Singing our burial songs, sad and low,
Each wondering who would be the next to go.

The young man swept his arms towards the skies
'It was a bomb, they tell us now,' he cried, raising sightless eyes,
'Pouring deathly rays over our sacred earth,
Poisoning forever our native land, our land of Dreamtime birth.'

We were expendable, no one takes the blame,
But let it go down in history to their everlasting shame.

———

The Royal Commission attempted to reconstruct the radiation dose received by the Aboriginal people around Wallatinna Station at the time. This included external and internal doses. The estimated total dose was 93.4 rem, but the contribution of the overall dose made by the particular diet of Aboriginals hunting for food, and consequent biological magnification that would have taken place, was ignored. (Note that the vomiting experienced by the people at Wallatinna Station is consistent with a dose of 80–100 rem in five to ten per cent of people exposed. However, this is not for people living in the open.) In its final analysis, the Royal Commission believed the Aboriginal explanation – with the qualification that the illnesses experienced could have been psychogenic and arising from the frightening experience, or could have been a combination of causes. It also concluded that there had been a failure to consider the distinctive lifestyles of the people. On reflection this seems an extraordinarily weak statement.

Currently the Aboriginal people of the Coober Pedy area are fighting the prospect of a nuclear waste dump on their country. Their Iratiwanti web site describes the effects of the radiation experienced in the 1950s.

From Kupa Piti Kungka Tjuta Declaration of Opposition:

[T]he Government used the Country for the Bomb. Some of us were living at Twelve Mile, just out of Coober Pedy. The smoke was funny and everything looked hazy. Everybody got sick. Other people were at Mabel Creek and many people got sick. Some people were living at Wallatinna. Other people got moved away. Whitefellas and all got sick. When we were young, no woman got breast cancer or any other kind of cancer. Cancer was unheard of. And no asthma either, we were people without sickness.

We've been fighting about it, the government for years. We know about the radioactivity, we were here with the bomb Emu/ Maralinga. We never saw our old people sick before this. They used to walk very long ways. After that, they were just dropping here and there, crippled, sick, short of breath. Died.

Turning now to those who were directly involved in the Emu bomb tests, Norman Geschke's account of the RAAF's involvement in tracking the radioactive cloud is remarkable. The men who flew in the Lincoln bombers that year were expendable. They were ordered to fly into highly contaminated and dangerous atmospheres. There would be no enemy search-lights tracking them, no anti-aircraft firing and no enemy airplanes chasing them, only the unseen 'bullets' of seemingly harmless dust.

Norman Geschke

In January 1953 I was posted to 82 Bomber Wing as its weapons officer. The Wing consisted of 3 Squadrons: 1, 2 and 6 Squadron, equipped with Lincoln aircraft which were four-engine heavy bombers.

I think it was about July of 1953 when some rumours began to circulate that the Wing was going to be employed on a special task, but it was still secret until the squadrons were deployed at Woomera and Richmond later in the year when the operation became known as 'Totem'. I flew as one of the aircraft captains with No. 2 Squadron and departed for Richmond on 27 September in Lincoln A73-21.

At Richmond, briefings were held and instructions given on the technique of tracking the radioactive cloud. The other technical sampling crew to fly with my crew were briefed as to their role but the main crew were not instructed on this. There was no instruction given on protection from radioactivity or protective clothing (of which there was none) nor was anything said about decontamination of flying suits, helmets or the crew. This was thought a little strange but the assurances were that protective clothing was unnecessary and there was no danger from radioactivity.

The plan for No. 2 Squadron was for one aircraft to take off as soon as the bomb was exploded and carry out background flights to deter-mine the ambient radioactive levels in the atmosphere before the radioactive cloud passed through the area. Other aircraft would then track the cloud and measure the radioactivity by means of inboard detection equipment and canisters carried on the outside of the aircraft.

A roster was drawn up with crews allotted time slots. The crew, which was allocated to the time slot when the bomb went off, would do the initial background flight. My crew won the jackpot for this and we took off as scheduled.

The next morning, other No. 2 Squadron aircraft took off at intervals to track the cloud and measure its radioactivity. The cloud's expected path was to be over northern New South Wales and Queensland. Later that day my crew was detailed to take up clean canisters to Townsville for the following day's tracking flights. Our route was planned to miss the cloud to avoid any chance of contaminating the clean canisters we were carrying.

However, owing to a navigational error by the crew of one of the tracking aircraft, the cloud had been plotted in the wrong position and the subsequent tracking aircraft could not locate it. A radioactive cloud is not visible like a normal weather cloud, and its presence is determined by sensing equipment rather like a Geiger counter.

At one point I noticed some unusual flickering on the radar screen and wondering what it was, I suggested that the radioation-sensing equipment be turned on. This was done and high readings obtained, indicating that we had entered the radioactive cloud. I have not been able to get a satisfactory explanation as to why the radar gave these unusual indications. Such indications were not noticed in the other aircraft that flew into the cloud. It was obvious that my aircraft, which should have been sent on a safe track, had inadvertently been sent on a track which intercepted the cloud.

Realising that the aircraft had entered the cloud, and as the cloud was obviously not where it was expected, it was desirable to determine its correct position, where it was heading and at what speed. There is a recommended procedure for tracking radioactive clouds. When a radioactive reading is obtained, the aircraft continues flying on its course until the reading ceases. Then an opposite course is flown, again entering the cloud and measuring the time taken before the aircraft exits the cloud on the other side. At this point, where the reading ceases, the aircraft returns back along its course for half the length of time taken to pass through the cloud on its previous heading. At this halfway point, a new course at 90 degrees is flown until the cloud is exited. A reverse course is flown, timing

P51 Mustang used to check damage in the Emu
tests (photo by Avon Hudson, 1960)

how long it takes to pass through the cloud. The position of the
aircraft at this time gives an indication of the centre of the cloud.

The procedure is repeated a few times and the cloud is plotted
during each procedure, giving a series of geographical location
points. From these points the position of the cloud is determined
as well as the speed and direction in which it is travelling.

After carrying out these procedures a few times and establishing
the correct position, speed and direction of the cloud, we flew on
to Townsville.

There was no decontamination procedure carried out and our
unlaundered flying clothes were worn the next day. At this time crews
were not unduly concerned because of the assurance given that there
would be no detriment or danger from flying through the radioactive
cloud. How wrong this assurance was! It was only much later that it
was realised that the crews should have been breathing full oxygen
instead of contaminated air, that the aircraft should have received
decontamination treatment before being flown again and that all
flying clothing should have been properly laundered.

Some 49 years later, after a lot of thought and with the knowledge that two and possibly three of my crew may have died of cancer due to their contact with the radioactive cloud, I seriously question the irresponsibility of a government, without fully analysing the risks, agreeing to send servicemen on such a mission. I also seriously question the British government and British scientists who conned the Australian government into agreeing to atomic tests which would imperil the troops and airman supporting the trials.

I am aware that the British seem to have little regard for their servicemen who have taken part in ill-conceived and ill-executed campaigns led by grossly incompetent generals. I am also aware that Australians have been inveigled to participate in these disasters, however, I would have hoped that Australian governments would have been wise to this cavalier attitude of the British before again committing Australian servicemen to unnecessary exposure to often deadly radioactivity.

What upsets me more is the immoral denial of the negligence by successive ministers and their cohorts who continue to stand in the way of servicemen and their widows seeking compensation. Servicemen were used as guinea pigs during the trials; no government has apologised and few, if any, servicemen or their widows or children have been compensated.

———

Over the years, many people have visited the Emu site even though it is a part of the Woomera restricted zone. The majority would not have known that there was any danger. This tells us something about the attitude of the Australian authorities towards Emu – it was just a small spot in the desert and wasn't worth bothering with.

Another Emu story comes from one of the few civilians who worked at Emu Field.

Pat Finch

As far as I am aware, there were only four Australian civilians sent to Emu. The only other civilians were British scientists. Of the four [Australians], I was probably the most junior. They were John Stannier photographer, Wally Jones engineer, Len Beadell surveyor and myself, the rocket man. Len Beadell and I were the only two of the four who were exposed to radiation. About ten years after that I was diagnosed with a thyroid problem, which I am told is the first thing to go from radiation.

Each small team had a specific job and was provided with a vehicle that they used without mercy. No drivers were provided to my knowledge. Our little team consisted of an Australian colonel, an English REME captain, a Welsh chemist, and myself. We had the job of firing rockets through the bomb cloud and collecting the filters from the noses of the rockets after they landed and rushing them back to Adelaide for analysis. My main job was looking after the rockets, loading them, setting them up for firing, and helping to recover the samples. Recovering the rockets began 20 minutes after the firing. This meant donning radiation suits and going within three to four kilometres of where the bomb had been exploded, and digging them out of the ground. It was hot work and not much fun! There was a problem with the first explosion (on 25 October). There was a wind shear and the radioactive cloud moved before the rockets arrived. The rockets missed the cloud. In order to get some samples a call was made for volunteers to walk across the bomb crater, to pick up earth from the crater surface (at ground zero). [It was precisely this explosion that caused the Black Mist. Was the wind shear associated with the observation that the Black Mist rolled low over the country?]

Our team volunteered, as it was our samples that were lost. Beadell also volunteered. So apart from the radiation that we may have received from digging out the rockets we were definitely exposed [to a large hazard] by walking across the crater a few weeks after the bomb had been fired.'

Our final story of the Emu fiasco tells about an army man, Warrant Officer William Cameron Jones who died of a rare bone marrow disease in 1966. He must have received massive doses of radiation. His widow, Audrey, received a paltry amount in compensation. The compensation was only made available because the nature of his disease was such that the Australian government could not deny that it was radiation-induced. We publish here a part of Audrey's letter to the Hon Bruce Scott, the then minister for Veterans' Affairs, dated 4 June 2001:

Recent newspaper and media reports have focused on Australians being used as 'guinea pigs' and the discoveries of researchers about the high incidence of specific disorders such as leukaemia and bone cancer among those present at the blasts.

My husband, Warrant Officer William Cameron Jones was at the tests coded 'Totem' at Emu Plains in 1953. During his term of service at the site he spent days with a tank used as experimental material during the blast. He wore no protective clothing and was never informed of any potential hazards because of exposure to radiation.

I cannot stress enough that my husband is not encountering medical disabilities now, in the year 2001 – he died in January 1966, at the age of 40 years – his illness had emerged in the early 60s. Like the well-documented radiation-induced illnesses of the Hibakusha – the survivors of Hiroshima and Nagasaki – my husband's disease surfaced a decade after the blast.

I can assure you that my husband suffered a most terrible illness. He, and his family around him, endured a period of time that should not be borne by anybody ... When Bill died his children were aged 18, 11, 7 and twins of 3 years.

The 11-year-old mentioned above, who was conceived shortly after his father's return from the atomic tests, died of carcinoma some 18 months ago after a long battle with the disease.

We rest our case.

4 – Monte Bello 1956: Operation Mosaic

The bombs were exploded on 16 May: 15 kilotons fired
at 11.50 am; 19 June: 60 kilotons fired 10.14 am

We now return to the Monte Bello Islands where the largest bomb explosion on Australian soil took place. It caused enormous contamination across the northern part of the country – right across to the Queensland coast and as far south as Alice Springs. In this chapter we present the accounts of two navy people, Bob Dennis and Douglas Brookes. Bob was at both the 1952 and 1956 explosions at Monte Bello. As a young sailor he had no idea of the dangers of radiation. Douglas was a young Australian seaman seconded to HMS *Alert*. He suffered great emotional trauma from being up close to an atomic bomb, similar to that experienced by survivors of the Hiroshima bombing.

Bob Dennis

In 1956 when I was 21 going on 22, I was the navigating officer on HMAS *Karangi*. [*Karangi* was a World War Two boom defence ship of about 400 tons that was used in Darwin Harbour, it had a maximum speed of about eight knots.] We didn't have too many mod cons on it and we were not fitted out with anything suitable for nuclear defence. We could not even wash down the ship and it had no hatches – and amazingly we did not have radar. I was the navigating officer, in the old tradition, using a compass. In the early stages our main job was to run out the stores from the town of Onslow to the Monte Bello Islands. We took all kinds of stores and

41

we also took personnel out there. We sailed into the lagoon in the Monte Bellos and anchored near the remains of HMS *Plym*. [*Plym* was the ship that housed the first atomic bomb that was detonated on the ship in 1952.]

We took out newspaper people and some of the (Australian) Safety Committee people such as Ernest Titterton and Leslie Martin.

I don't remember much about the earliest explosion. We were there but that has gone from my memory. I think we were on our way back from Onslow to the Monte Bellos when it happened and we were probably about 80 miles away. In fact we were 'savage' on the fact that we missed out on the first one. For the next one, the big one, we were probably only 20 miles away, to the south-east I think. I remember a signal coming through to 'GO – get out of the area as quickly as possible', because the wind had changed just before the explosion. It seemed like a bit of a panic, but at eight knots you can't go very far in a hurry. We ended up being in the path of the radiation cloud but I don't think it went right over the top of us. Then we went back into the lagoon at Monte Bello a few days after the explosion.

We were the first back into the lagoon by nearly a day. What struck us as amusing was one of HMS *Narvik*'s boats came in [the *Narvik* was a British boat] with guys dressed in white suits. We had a bit of a laugh about their protective suits when they first came in – we thought 'oh yer'. At that age and not knowing anything about the dangers, what more could you expect? These were the physicists. After that, HMS *Narvik* herself came into the lagoon, as did HMS *Alert*.

I was in charge of a group of about 20 British Royal Marines and engineers. With the aid of a landing craft we went ashore each day, leaving about 8 am to salvage any pieces of equipment that still worked from around ground zero – such as generators and jeeps. These were all dismantled by the engineers and brought back on board HMAS *Karangi* as deck cargo. I remember there was dust everywhere. The equipment was eventually transhipped across to Maralinga.

None of the physicists gave us any warnings when we walked over ground zero – a circular area of about 800 yards in radius. The sand was black and brittle like thin flakes stuck together. When you walked on it, it would crack open to reveal the fused soil and sand. We had no idea whether it was dangerous or not. Actually, we had no knowledge whatsoever of radioactivity! Our protective clothing was pretty simple – a pair of shorts, cap and a pair of sandals, but no shirt because it was too hot. The British Royal Marines were in the same situation wearing the same clothing. It took about three days to complete the salvaging work and there were no wash down procedures. Of course, we went in the sea for our own enjoyment and we caught fish to eat. No one told us that you shouldn't swim in the lagoon or catch fish, so we thought it was okay.

Not long after the second explosion we took a very sick scientist, Dr Eddy, from Monte Bello to Onslow [He was one of the Australian Safety Committee members and he died shortly afterwards].

No one warned us about anything, and as far as I know the Captain wasn't warned either. In our officers' mess there were only three of us, the Captain, myself, and a commissioned bosun [warrant officer on a warship who is responsible for the maintenance of the ship] from the Royal Navy, and I cannot remember any discussion about warnings. We were in the lagoon for three to four days. I guess then the Brits organised a big lash-up party on HMS *Alert* for all the officers and scientists. The only contact we had with the white-coated scientists was at that dinner. Two days later everyone departed. We departed south and I think we had HMAS *Fremantle* with us.

The whole thing from my point of view, and I would suggest most people's, was bloody boring – even between the two explosions it was boring. One curious thing was the radioactivity measuring film badges we wore. We were not told anything, we used to hand back the badges every second day or so – we got them off the boffins on HMS *Narvik* – the Brits kept them and that was that. After the loading was finished we steamed away to Onslow to refuel. On the way back to Fremantle we had shelter in Shark Bay due to bad weather. I left the ship, I think it was the 5 or 6 July, in Fremantle.

I didn't think any more about the trip until a few years later while doing a few courses that included information on radioactivity. I realised things weren't as they should have been on our ship. We should have been equipped for things like wash downs.

At times I felt lethargic but I was a reservist until 1978 when I went on the retired list. I moved on with my life and I didn't think any more about being at Monte Bello until I watched a programme on Channel 9's 60 Minutes programme in 1982 or 1983. They interviewed Mr Howard Beale who had been the Minister for Supply at the time. He got up there and said all Australian servicemen at the Monte Bello tests were supplied with protective clothing. I got very angry over this – I rang Channel 9 and said this was rubbish. But I never heard anything from them. This turned my whole thinking around. I asked myself what other lies were being told about what was going on up there? Why is he saying that?

My wife knows how furious I was – it suddenly all came back to me. I found out about the Nuclear Veterans' Association and I joined up. I have been told that a number of the crew suffered from cancer-related diseases.

I appeared before the Royal Commission in 1985. The Commission asked me a series of questions that I tried to answer as best I could. Since 1985–1986, I don't care what anyone says, we were used as 'guinea pigs'. We were counted as expendable. It just annoys me, and it was never discussed in the navy. It seems it became a closed book; as if it never happened.

It annoys me that all of the governments since those days have not given us any recognition. They don't care that people were exposed to dangerous radiation and quite a considerable hazard. I'm not after monetary compensation but I think we should at least be recognised. No one seems to want to admit it. I don't think anyone wants to be running around with medals on their chest, but what I would like to see is that everyone who was involved be subject to the repatriation benefit that is available to other servicemen, such as the Gold Card. Just because it wasn't considered a theatre of war and we weren't being shot at doesn't mean we were not at grave risk – as it happens you can't see radiation coming at you! It is a bit of an anomaly in a lot of regards because some people who were in a theatre of war are eligible even though they have never been exposed to any danger. To me, the fairest thing would be to give us repatriation benefits. I'm not looking at damages.

Looking back, the worst thing about the whole affair was that we weren't told. Perhaps then we could have been made aware of how we could have reduced the risks with wash downs and decent masks. The government betrayed us because they didn't tell us nor did they provide any equipment to help us – it was a betrayal of trust. We were put in the way of extreme danger and we were not prepared in any way to minimise it – we were young, happy-go-lucky and ignorant about the whole thing.

––––––

Why were the British scientists given protective gear and yet the servicemen left unprotected? This is more than negligence. The navy personnel were handed radiation exposure badges and these were regularly exchanged, so the authorities were monitoring the levels of radiation received by the men. If there was a real purpose in monitoring, it follows that the Australian Safety Committee and the British Bomb Group must have been concerned about the possibility of high levels of exposure. They knew there was a risk when sending men into the site of an atomic bomb test.

The size of this bomb test was enormous compared to all the other tests in Australia. Officially, and belatedly, the AWRE were induced to say it was equivalent to 60 kilotons, but this was a massive bomb – and in fact was more than 90 kilotons. And yet they allowed British and Australian armed forces personnel to wander over the site retrieving a few measly pieces of equipment – a minute saving in material cost compared with the cost of the whole exercise – and at what potential human cost? It doesn't add up. But what if the real reason was to see what dose of radiation men received while working in such an environment within a week or so of the blast? That would be useful knowledge indeed. It might answer the questions about whether men could work in a war under such conditions and it might shed light on the radiological effects.

Douglas Brooks

My involvement, as a serving member in the Royal Australian Navy, during Operation 'Mosaic' at the Monte Bello Islands, came after I was seconded to HMS *Alert*. She was a submarine frigate attached to the Far Eastern Fleet of the Royal Navy. Her role during this operation was one of logistical support along with many other ships and small craft.

I joined HMS *Alert* in Hong Kong in late March 1956 and I found my sea legs on our way to Singapore where the store ship was located. Arriving in Malaysian waters placed us within the continuing conflict of the Malaya 'Emergency'. I was not too perplexed about the high risk of involvement but I remained rather suspicious of the fact that I had not yet been told of the purpose of my hasty draft from Australia to HMS *Alert*. Storing our ship in Singapore was a rather drawn-out exercise, we appeared to be provisioning for an extended time at sea, plus our full ship's complement of sailors had not yet been realised due to the fact that we had placed some members of our crew ashore, prior to our departure from Hong Kong. These were Chinese sailors who were normally engaged by the Royal Navy aboard their Far Eastern station vessels. This action, in itself, raised some concern as to the increasingly covert movements of our ship.

Leaving Singapore came as a relief – after being shot at by a Communist terrorist. We still had no announcement from our skipper as to our modus operandi. The senior ratings began to question every aspect of our departure from the normal routine. As the most junior crew-member at sea, aged 18, I put my faith in those above me.

Passing through the Sunda Straits on Monday 26 March, our ship continued on a southerly course. Immediately following our entry into the open sea, our skipper cleared the lower deck and announced our final destination and the purpose of the operation.

Morale went into sharp decline. Being exposed to atomic testing was not an attractive thought. It conjured up thoughts of becoming sterile before manhood knocked on the door! Nevertheless, we were serving members of Her Majesty's Navy and subject to the Queen's Regulations and Admiralty Instructions. We duly arrived at the Monte Bello Islands on Friday 30 March.

Douglas Brooks

The captain reported that once we were stationed at the Monte Bello Islands, 15 scientists were to be accommodated on the ship. This extra load and the fact that on average, 12 hands were to be provided as manpower for work ashore (the operation was behind schedule due to a cyclone that delayed the arrival of HMS *Narvik* by about five days) meant that the whole ship's company suffered to a considerable degree. On 6 April the *Alert* sailed for Onslow and the captain reported that the amount of beer consumed at the one Onslow public house the evening of arrival, ranked as an all time record for Onslow. The *Alert* was back at Monte Bello shortly after and the First Sea Lord, First Earl of Mountbatten of Burma, paid a quick visit. He addressed the ship's companies of HMS *Alert*, HMS *Narvik* and HMAS *Fremantle*. The sailors were not allowed to go onto Trimouille Island as it was still radioactive from the 1952 bomb test.

Lord and Lady Mountbatten – Monte
Bello, Western Australia

I began to question the wisdom of the British Empire and reflect on
my past period of recruit training which was still fresh in my mind,
[when] we were shown large and graphic depictions of the devastation
from the Hiroshima and Nagasaki atomic bombs. The term 'guinea
pigs' began to worry me. It was an expression that conjured up fears
and mistrust of how we might be used. It began to invade my mind
and fester there as I thought about all the possibilities. 'Surely,'
I thought, 'I am not going to be exposed to this madness!' And, 'Just
how long and how much of the experimentation do I have to endure?'
Our cameras were confiscated and censure of letter writing came
into effect immediately following our arrival off the Monte Bello Islands.

Film badges were issued to all of the crew-members. These were
to be worn day and night. I attempted to explain that the film badges
were of such frail construction that they would fall apart in a matter
of days. And, if I was to receive any level of ionising radiation, I sure
as hell wanted something more reliable to record it. This was met
with a curt response.

Being at anchor with easy access to many of the islands of

the Monte Bello group served as an ideal platform for viewing the activities ashore. Construction work appeared to be well advanced. I took special note of a large tent that had been erected on a raised section of a beach, later discovering that this canvas expanse was to be known as 'The Lido' and would provide for rest and recreation for off-duty periods. A cold beer or two was available at a nominal charge. During my first opportunity to be on the beach at The Lido I found to my amazement, roped off areas carrying signs warning of certain levels of contamination from the 1952 Test – 'Operation Hurricane – making times ashore more akin to risk than recreation.

Activity gradually increased on and around the islands. The arrival of various types of craft during the next few days made it most evident that this operation was developing into an exercise of some magnitude. Meteorologic structures and distillation plants took shape. The Royal Marine Engineers erected the tower that would cradle the atomic device named 'G1' at the northern end of Trimouille Island.

During this time life aboard ship worsened. It is not surprising that morale continued to decline. Talk of desertion circulated. The captain informed crew-members of the penalties when Queen's Regulations and Admiralty Instructions were contravened. Within days of this warning, two crew members went AWOL when we were tied up at the small port of Onslow. This port, south of the islands, was our pick-up point for both of the firing mechanisms of the two bombs (G1 and G2) – they were ferried out from the UK aboard Royal Air Force flights.

On 16 May I was ordered to my 'action station', positioned in a magazine below deck, therefore, my visual contact with the actual blast was curtailed. However, I knew the detonation of G1 was imminent. The questions I asked myself were: 'Why close up at action stations? Surely we are not going to be that close to the detonation?' Within an hour my mounting fears were realised as I sweated and strained to supply the demand for projectiles to the forward gun mount. The bulkheads of the magazine shook with the shock wave of the explosion. The shock wave of G1 – travelling underwater – reached the ship easily as we were positioned only nine miles from ground zero.

The forward upper deck
of HMS Alert

My immediate response was to vacate my action station. But I stood firm, aware of the penalties I would incur if I deserted my post. Sweating profusely and in a state of uncontrolled shaking, I awaited orders for stand-down from the action stations. Rejoining my shipmates above deck came as an enormous relief, but their description of the detonation and the ensuing mushroom cloud did nothing to allay my growing fears.

Following the detonation of G1, the weather pattern changed considerably. Winds became unpredictable and sea conditions worsened, disrupting the preparations for the second detonation. The window of opportunity for the Brits to explode the second bomb was fast running out. The 'buzz' on board that pervaded the mess-decks was that G2 would go ahead even if the prevailing winds were not favourable.

The morning of 19 June dawned with what appeared to be near-perfect weather conditions. Finally, the countdown could commence – it appeared that the British were determined to explode the bomb. [By far the largest bomb ever exploded in Australia, we now know it was a massive bomb of around 98 kilotons, some eight times the size of the Hiroshima bomb.]

Standing on the forward upper deck (fo'c'sle) and dressed only in our blue shorts, underwear and sandals I listened intently to the continuing countdown that was conveyed over the ship's tannoy system (loud-speaker system). At minus ten seconds, orders came for us to turn our backs and cover our eyes with our hands and not to turn to face the blast for about eight seconds. Ground zero lay ten flat miles to the north. Immediately following the issue to fire the bomb, I experienced an enormous flash of intense burning bright light. I could see the bones of my hands as I covered my eyes – as if they were being x-rayed. A great sheet of heat burnt the backs of our necks. Soon after, an enormous clap of deafening thunder rolled over the ship. This was followed by a shock wave of high intensity that shook the frigate to such a degree that I lost my footing on the steel deck. With the order to turn round and face north, I found myself staring with disbelief at a gigantic mushroom cloud. A fireball rose upward through its stem with increasing speed. At the base of the mushroom's stem walls, what I can only visually liken to molten glass spread out in all directions. Billowing up and outwards, the cloud continued to form, attaining a very high altitude in a very short time.

Within minutes my attention was drawn to the clear skies surrounding the mushroom cloud's apex and appearing out to the east were two aircraft. They slowly converged on the cloud. One after the other they disappeared momentarily then emerged from the western side of the cloud, then altered course and went south. Still reeling from what I had seen and the effects of what I had felt, I paused to reflect on the safety, or otherwise, of the crew aboard those two aircraft.

The mushroom cloud continued to rise and then, quite suddenly, commenced to disperse, its formation altering as the winds sent it in an easterly direction. 'This cannot be correct,' I said to myself. We were informed that the fallout would be carried out to sea to the west, where HMS *Diana* was positioned on station in preparation to test her wash-down gear. [The easterly course of the radioactive plume was to take the radioactive fallout right across the top of Australia.]

Within hours of the dispersal of the mushroom cloud, the *Alert* got underway. Of course, I thought we had finished with the madness and would be heading out of the area. Much to my dismay we continued towards ground zero. Our passage through the channel was eerie. The sight of hundreds of floating dead fish drifting on an opaque jade sea turned my stomach. Cautiously approaching the land mass, which was still 'red hot' from the detonation, our ship dropped anchor close to the beach. I did not recognise this location as its profile had been completely altered by the explosion. What remained was a molten mess of rock with clouds of what looked like sulfur steam rising up and dispersing into the sea.

As I mustered to assist in the launch of the ship's cutter, I pondered on the insanity of those preparing to venture ashore to retrieve instrumentation. Apart from the obvious hazards now evident I wondered just how 'hot' this area was. As the cutter headed towards the beach, I was amazed to see its occupants were only clad in white overalls and boots – surely this was crazy?

Within the hour, the cutter could be seen returning to the ship with crew members waving frantically from its bow. Shouts of distress conveyed the fact that they had come into contact with contaminated flotsam. Panic immediately broke out aboard ship, and orders were relayed to rig sea-horses to facilitate the wash-down of the cutter. Geiger counters were produced from below decks and were handed out. As I assisted with the cutter's retrieval and it was swung aboard on its davits, the Geiger counters commenced to register alarming levels of radioactive contamination. My reaction was one of alarm and helplessness. The wash-down began, but the absence of any decontamination procedures for the cutter crew and occupants was evident. I failed to comprehend the blasé approach of the officers and reflected on my basic training when I was taught about some of the dangers of ionising radiation and its effect on human health.

Fear about the ramifications of this insane event commenced to haunt me and an intense hatred of the service began to manifest itself. Other crew members felt the same and talk of desertion pervaded the mess-deck again. Somehow the navy didn't seem like such a good career option after all. I began to calculate the remaining time of my service.

Leaving the Monte Bello Islands came as a relief to us all. There was no debriefing or talk about what had been going on during the previous few months. The ship's captain became isolated and there was talk of him suffering from ill health. Discussion below decks turned to the probability of the contamination of our food and water resources. We relied on making our own fresh water from the ship's desalination equipment, and this made us prone to the radioactive contamination in the surrounding sea water. Even our fresh-vegetable lockers were located above decks and subject to airborne ionised particles.

By the time we reached Singapore I was most anxious to sever my ties with this British ship and return to Australia. But this took a few days as our contingent was required to be in transit at HMS *Terror*. This naval base provided some respite from the harsh and emotionally draining experiences at the Monte Bello Islands. Of the 26 Australians on that ship, only two of us are left alive. Later, when I heard that the Australian scientists of the Safety Committee had reported to the press that there was absolutely no danger from the radioactive cloud of the huge explosion that I had witnessed, I lost all faith and trust in scientists and the government. I am still awaiting an answer to the question: 'Why did they put us virtually underneath an atomic bomb explosion?' The only rational answer I can think of is that we were guinea pigs. If that is true, as I am sure it is, God help humanity.

Arriving home on leave I found myself becoming withdrawn and unable to relate my harrowing experiences to my immediate family. They did not press me for any details relating to my months of absence – so I saw no point in talking about them. On returning to land-based duties following my leave, I found that my sleeping patterns became erratic and I took to drinking heavily and became quite detached from all aspects of navy life. I had nightmares, flashbacks, night sweats and insomnia. These have continued for years. I lost contact with my fellow shipmates from the *Alert*, the only men who would understand and be able to help each other, and I discovered I could not relate to other people who did not share my experiences. I was irreconcilably changed by the experiences with the bomb. The remaining years of my service were spent attached to the Fleet Air Arm; I saw service in the Far East Strategic Reserve in Malaya during the emergency. I never felt the same about the service after the life-changing event of the bomb.

I went back into civilian life in 1962 and I am afraid my dependence on alcohol increased. Nightmares became a part of my everyday life and in 1991 I suffered a mental breakdown, was diagnosed with Post Traumatic Stress Disorder and underwent psychiatric treatment. The same year I was told that I had an untreatable bone disease. Sadie, my wife of 37 years, has been a most wonderful support – because it affected our relationship deeply. Today, with the support of psychiatric counselling, I manage to cope most of the time and I try not to think of those few months in 1956 when at the age of 18, my view of the world was distorted and changed forever. My wife Sadie is quite right when she says the veterans have to keep on fighting against the injustices and the contempt with which our lives are held. Someone must be made accountable for all that has happened, for the lives that have been destroyed and the lies that have been told so often. As a postscript which shows that what has happened to me (and others) will not end with our passing, my daughter has been diagnosed with the same bone disease that I have!

––––––

Douglas's story is an insight into the emotional effect of the bomb testing that was carried out at the Monte Bello Islands. The survivors of the Hiroshima and Nagasaki atomic bombs experienced similar effects, some developing a psychological condition known as 'hibakusha'. Psychiatrist Robert Lifton has described this condition as a form of 'psychic numbing' – enabling the survivor to defend himself against the understandable anxiety of death and, in the case of Operation Mosaic, the horror of participating in an experiment to test the effectiveness of a weapon of mass destruction. Even if the 19 June bomb was only 60 kilotons, that is still five times greater than the bomb that was dropped on Hiroshima. It is not surprising then, that the witnesses should suffer from traumatic psychological conditions. And all for the sake of advancing science and power.

'Hibakusha' means 'atomic bomb survivor'. In Japan it includes not only the direct survivors of Hiroshima and Nagasaki but also people who lived further away or entered the destroyed cities soon after the bombing. The horror of the bombing is a shared experience and often survivors are unable to talk about their experiences because they are beyond description and too painful to remember. Many suffer a deep sense of guilt because they ran away and did not stay to help less fortunate victims.

While the situation for the Australian (and British) servicemen was not the same, there are parallels in the burying of the trauma of the events witnessed and the psychological impact of the overwhelming experiences.

5 – Maralinga 1956: Operation Buffalo

The bombs were exploded on 27 September: 15 kilotons
fired at 5 pm; 4 October: 1.5 kilotons fired at 4.30 pm;
11 October: 3 kilotons fired at 2.27 pm; 22 October:
10 kilotons fired at 12.05 am

In this chapter we meet a number of people involved in
Operation Buffalo. Peter Webb was at Maralinga from August
to October 1956. He was a member of the military who was
deliberately exposed to the worst of the blast. Edward 'Ted'
Bell was working in the area from 1954–1963, as a member of
the Federal police force. Ted signed the *Official Secrets Act*,
so exactly how close he got to ground zero is not known. He
became a very sick man. Patricia Donnelly suffered the loss of
her father and brother as a result of the tests. Joseph Baker and
Gary Ryan were both unaware of the harmful effects of ionising
radiation. They, like so many others, were taken for granted.
Peter W Harvey of Burra, South Australia, was working as an
editorial journalist for the *News*, Adelaide's evening newspaper
at the time of the tests. On a fateful day in October 1956, he
became embroiled in a controversy that would end his career
as a journalist and shake the confidence and complacency of the
Menzies Government. Brian Potter was a young CSIRO scientist
working at the Division of Biochemistry and General Nutrition
in Adelaide. His boss in Adelaide was Hedley Marston, the only
senior Australian scientist to try and stop the bomb tests. His
account comes from a statement he sent to the Department of
Primary Industries and Energy in Canberra in 1988.

Approach to Maralinga Village

Peter Webb

I was posted to Maralinga from the First Battalion Royal Australian Regiment when I was a 20-year-old private. The Regiment was stationed in Queensland in 1956, and six of us were told that we were going to South Australia. We didn't have the faintest idea why! We went down to Keswick Barracks in Adelaide and we stayed there about a week or a fortnight. We noticed that troops were coming in from different units – like the Royal Australian Engineers. Eventually, on 26 August we all went down to the railway station and caught 'The Tea and Sugar Train' to Watson Siding, then to a place called 11 Mile Camp.

This camp took in all of the indoctrinee officers from England, Australia and Canada. There were about 67 of us at 11 Mile Camp and about 20–25 were Australians. The majority were British National Servicemen. Our job was to build and service the camp, which became a tent city. After a while, more and more indoctrinees moved in. I would say we had about 250–300 men. They were a floating population, so eventually the total number that passed through would have been around 1000. The bigwig boss of the bomb project, Sir William Penney, was also there.

We soon learned, on the grapevine, why we were there; the British were going to do some more atomic bomb tests. Before the atomic bombs were let off they took us up to ground zero to have a look around. We saw the tanks, Super Marine Swift aircraft, trucks and lots of ordnance of all types spread around. Strangely, although we were only the support group for 11 Mile Camp, we were treated as if we were indoctrinees, except of course, they did not allow us to go to the lectures that were being put on for the officers as part of their indoctrination. All we were told was that there was nothing to worry about. In the army when something is called 'Operation' it is classified as hazardous and the 1956 bomb tests were called 'Operation Buffalo'. That makes you think!

Just before the first bomb was exploded it started to rain, the Brits were furious – raining in the desert! So we continued to sleep soundly until the early hours of 27 September when we went up to the bomb site at a place they called One Tree Hill. There were about 250 men, all officers except about ten ratings, not counting the truck drivers. We stood around gazing at the sunrise when an officer came up and said, 'This will be a ground burst on a tower,' and so we looked at a tower about seven to ten miles away and said, 'That's it' and he said, 'No – that is it right in front of you' – under a mile away. It has taken 45 years for the government to admit that we were under a mile away. All I was wearing were my shorts, short-sleeve shirt, my army boots and a leather jerkin – British Army issue.

We were told to turn our backs to the bomb, close our eyes and cover them with our hands. There was a countdown from ten to zero and then a brilliant flash, and I saw an X-ray of my hands. A great blast of heat hit my back, I heard a deafening noise, and a dust storm passed through our ranks. When we turned around there was what seemed like a dark-brown mound with red flames flashing through it, and in a few minutes it started to form the mushroom cloud, and all the dust and ground rubbish that had blown out through our ranks on the initial detonation, was sucked back through us and into the mushroom cloud as it formed.

We sat there covered in dust with everything flowing over us. I have no idea how much radiation we copped, but we did have dosimeters on to check our exposure. The mushroom cloud gradually formed and then the Canberra jets flew through it, collecting radioactive samples. Then a funny thing happened; an eagle flew through the cloud. This caused great excitement and they sent a helicopter to catch it and see if it was affected by the radiation. I thought, at the time, how stupid chasing an eagle. But later I realised they were not so stupid as I began to understand what was going on. [If they caught the bird they could have measured the radioactivity on the feathers and the radioactivity it had ingested.] We sat there for three to four hours while the cloud drifted way and disintegrated.

Then we went to ground zero, right into the crater – the ground had turned to glass because of the heat. I thought I would like to get a bit of it so I gave it a kick with my boots but I couldn't chip any off. It was like concrete. The officers in charge told us to have a good look around so, not thinking about the dangers, we crawled round Centurion tanks and trucks and picked up ammunition that had been scattered everywhere. All the planes had their backs broken just behind the cockpit. The tanks were what they called 'hot', but they could have gone into active service again. The guns were rolled over and the trucks were crumpled up and thrown all over the place. There was a lot of damage and debris everywhere and some of the bunkers that had been built had collapsed. We were there for an hour or two looking around; sadly, we were not allowed to take souvenirs or photographs. When we went back to 11 Mile Camp we were not told to have a shower, but they did collect our film badges in a bucket. They're little square things with a bit of film inside – the darker it is the more radioactivity you have been exposed to. They told us they would let us know the results, but of course they didn't. I think we found out later that many of the dosimeters didn't work anyway. So we never got any information about our level of exposure to radiation. We went back to ground zero at One Tree Hill three to four times during the next week.

We had officers coming in and going all the time, having a look at the damage – they were the indoctrination forces. I wasn't a proper indoctrinee because I wasn't allowed to go and listen to the lectures where they were telling the officers about nuclear warfare. But when that bomb went off you didn't have to be an Einstein to work out what it was all about.

A couple of weeks later, on 4 October, they called us out again and we went up to the ground burst at Marcoo. This time I was in a bunker, again about 1000 yards from ground zero. It was really just a slit trench with walls of galvanised iron and no head cover. There were two British officers and myself in it when the bomb went off. Some other officers got into a Centurion tank. We were in contact with ground control by a field telephone and they told us to sit with our backs against the wall nearest the bomb and carry out the same drill as at One Tree Hill – close eyes and cover with hands. There was a vivid flash with the same X-ray results, the heat and the blast, and we were covered with rubbish. It all came into the trench and covered us. After this we stood up and had a look. I was surprised to see big boulders, as big as houses, scattered about the place. There was an English major there and I said to him: 'What if one of those rocks had of landed on this bunker?' He answered: 'They would have chipped your army number and name on it because they wouldn't have moved the rock.'

We came out of Maralinga at the end of October 1956 – so I saw all four explosions but only two close up. When we left I didn't think about what had happened for a long time. I just got on with life, initially being a soldier. In 1964, I had a skin complaint and I told the doctor that I had been at Maralinga. He said to me: 'Young fella, do not mention Maralinga – otherwise you will be like a leper, they don't want to know about you.' I struck that from different doctors. Some of them thought I had had a heart attack and they did tests but could not come up with anything. Later when I mentioned my service to another doctor, he said: 'You should have told us you was at Maralinga – there would have been an entirely different set of tests done on you.' He then said: 'I advise you not to have any children.' I got married in 1972 and told my wife that we must not have a family in case I pass on a genetic mutation to the next generation.

One day my wife Audrey noticed a freckle in the middle of my back and tried to make me go to the doctor. So one night when she was out I went round to see the doctor. I was immediately sent to a specialist, and he found three spots. I had to go into hospital straight away and have them cut out – they took a 12-inch melanoma between the shoulder blades – it was like the roots of a tree. It left a big dent in my back. Everything I have suffered has been on my back, never on my front – but then I did have my back to the radioactive blast.

The thing is I feel sorry for those people who do not have a Gold Card (I do because I saw war service in Korea) and for the people who have lost their fathers or husbands. The government must issue a one-off Gold Card to the wives of the men who served at the tests.

The government only wants me to go away and die. I am not wanted, and they will not accept their responsibility.

Edward Bell by Dorothy Bell

Edward Bell was an 'honest man' who served his country as a soldier in the Australian Infantry and later as a member of the Federal police force. Edward, who was more commonly known as Ted, believed in serving his country and did so without question or complaint, not knowing that the government that served the people of this country would be the instrument that turned a healthy man into a man whose medical record files read like a who's who of 'non-diagnosis'.

Ted, my husband, passed away ten years ago. He joined the Peace Officer Guard in December of 1954, leaving the army that he had served since 1941. On joining the Peace Officers he was immediately sent to Woomera as part of the force dealing with security on the Woomera Rocket Range and at Maralinga and Emu Field.

Ted was sent to X200, Emu and Maralinga during the tests from 1954–1963. He spent most of his service stationed at Woomera and at the Maralinga site while testing occurred. Being the man he was, and having signed the secrecy oath, Ted never talked about what really happened, but skirted around the stories till after he left the Federal police force. His stories even then were only for his family.

I recall his stories of the mushroom clouds, believing that Ted and the family were in no danger. He talked about so-called 'clean' and 'dirty' bombs. He also spoke of the men around him and some of the strange things that were happening to them: rashes, sickness and unexplained illnesses. How only the men that went down to the explosion site had protective gear and everyone else wore shorts as they were told there was no danger. However, windstorms in central Australia are not to be taken lightly; the red dust carrying nuclear activity was deposited all over South Australia.

He continually lost the use of the right side of his body until he passed away. Headaches, and unaccountable aches through his body accompanied by tiredness and dizzy spells, along with an anal itch that affected many of the men, made his life unbearable at times. Growths in joints were to follow him for 30 years. In 1978, after losing the use of his right side once again, he was examined by the Commonwealth Medical Officer (at the 'very old age' of 54). He was told 'what do you expect; you are an old man and should expect deterioration of your body'!

There have been dramatic advancements in medical diagnosis since the 1960s but when Ted passed away in 1992 there was still no diagnosis. His heart stopped, his body was discoloured in parts and there were strange growths on joints, but there were still no answers for a man who believed in serving his country. The cause of death was given as cardiomyopathy (idiopathic). In layman's terms, his heart stopped but we don't know why. He was a hypochondriac according to three leading medical specialists, despite his body showing conclusive evidence that something was happening and radiation had invaded a healthy man.

Our five children have not walked away unscarred. Some carry problems associated with radiation exposure, such as detached retinas, while others have unexplained illnesses that specialists with today's modern diagnostic equipment cannot answer. Six of his grandchildren and possibly his great-grandchildren have also been left legacies. There is no evidence in family history to account for these anomalies.

The legacy is not just physical but emotional. My second daughter would like to be a grandmother but she gets a knot inside her and she says prayers and hopes that she is never blessed – in case her grandchildren carry a legacy. My eldest girl has had to face her fears as each of her grandchildren has been born. Our youngest, born in

Woomera, decided early in her teens never to have children, through fear of the possible consequences.

Ted was a hero – he loved his country and he loved his family. But I also know the pain he felt for his children and grandchildren, who were given a legacy of 'non-diagnosis' by a government and system that wants to forget that he and others ever existed.

I continue to research every article I can find for Ted's sake. I fight for answers and proper recognition from the government.

Civilians at Maralinga by Patricia Donnelly

I have been deeply affected by Maralinga; I lost my dear father and brother because of what happened up there. They were both blissfully ignorant of the potential hazards and they became sick and died. I have been thinking about why this happened and trying to piece together some of the answers for years. This is why I am representing the civilian workers and their families. I know the men of the Australian armed forces need compensation and recognition for their service to the country, but the other men, the civilians, have sometimes been forgotten. They worked in some very hazardous situations and they too need recognition. I have made contact with a large number of civilian workers – many of whom feel angry and let down by successive Australian governments. The letters I have received are from people who knew no better at the time of their work at Maralinga. The recurring theme of their letters has been sadness and anger over the trust they placed in the authorities who sent them to Maralinga. These people never imagined that they would have been placing themselves at risk. They were, they feel, just pawns in the game of power. In many cases it wasn't until after they returned from their work at Maralinga that they realised there was something sinister about the experience – that they may have been exposed to a deadly, unseen hazard. Often this realisation was brought on by the fact that they left for Maralinga well and on their return became sick – often desperately so.

Remember, many were very young and many were blackmailed by the WRE authorities into spending time up there; there was no option for those who did not want to lose their job with WRE.

When you compare the military with the civilians you can say that on the one hand they were ordered up to one of the bomb sites, on the other hand some were forced by an unscrupulous employer.

Owen and Terry Donnelly by Patricia Donnelly

My father, Owen Donnelly, was a wonderful man. He was a great friend of many people, a good husband, and a fabulous dad. He and I were very close. We returned to Australia from England, for the second time in 1956, Dad returning before us. He got a job as a driver with the Weapons Research Establishment at Salisbury and soon my brother Terry joined him there.

Before long Dad said that he had to go to Maralinga. All the drivers took it in turn to go up there, so off he went the next day. It was a case of 'If you don't go, don't bother coming back to work here.' Then Terry organised to go as well because you could earn good money – not bad for a lad just arriving in a new country. As it turned out he stayed for about three months in the offices, and seemed to enjoy the company of all the lads from UK doing their National Service there.

Dad ended up telling the bosses he was coming home as his family had only been together for a week when he had been sent up to Maralinga, and he wanted to get home with us. He had only been there about three to four weeks, so of course that did not go down well and he was told: 'Well you find your own way home, we are not going to fly you back.' So Dad packed his bag and set off walking. As he walked he came upon Lenny Beadell's camp. Lenny gave Dad a wonderful meal; Dad said he had never had a steak that hung over both sides of the plate before. Next day he walked to Watson railway siding and slept there while awaiting a train. He arrived home three days later. He was very burnt, and he said he had been like that for a couple of weeks; it wasn't just the walking in the sun. He was covered in blisters, and they took a good few weeks to clear up and left scars.

Life was just fine for about 12 months; we even went on holiday camping. Dad bought a Holden car. It was his pride and joy; so much better than the old Vauxhall he had when we arrived.

Owen Donnelly

Then things started to go wrong. About October 1958, Dad started getting terrible pains in his stomach. It was put down to ulcers from the trauma of being away from the family for so long. We couldn't understand Dad being sick; he was never sick, except for bronchitis now and then. He didn't drink or smoke. Mum always gave us good healthy food – none of this quick 'take-away' stuff. But the pains continued and the doctors decided to investigate.

On my 16th birthday in January 1959, Dad had his first operation. It turned out to be cancer of the stomach, and the doctors took nearly all of his stomach away. It was devastating, and we were all in shock. I had never heard of cancer and not many other people had either. Dad was very fit and made a fairly good recovery, and he went back to work doing light driving. We were so pleased and you couldn't wipe the smile off Mum's face. They were so close.

Things started to look good again but around July, Dad started to have more pain and lost a lot of weight. The first operation in January was just a band-aid job. When Dad went into Calvary Hospital in July, doctors opened him up and the cancer was all through him, so now it was just a matter of time. It was the first time I had ever seen my big strong dad cry. He just couldn't believe it when the doctors told him; he hung onto all of us. He started on a new treatment called 'Cobalt' but it was too late. He came home in August and the first thing he did was hobble to the garage to see his beloved car. It wasn't there much longer; it was repossessed and that didn't help. Dad was to have this Cobalt every day so different people used to take him into Adelaide, usually the priests. They were very good.

Dad stayed home, usually in bed because he was very weak with this treatment and it made him vomit all the time. It was terrible sitting in the kitchen eating tea and he would try a little bit then he would vomit it all back up again. He went from being such a big strong man to skin and bones. He just sat in bed every day with his rosary beads and telling us how sorry he was that he had put us through so much in the last eight years.

Mum kept working for a while then decided that she wasn't going to leave him on his own any more. So she went on leave without pay. Dad had used up his little bit of sick leave he had from WRE. I was working in the library at WRE. Terry was planning to get married so he was saving every penny and just paying a bit for board. I didn't see my pay, it went straight on bills and a bit of food, and many times we had no food in the house at all. Things went from bad to worse with Dad's health, with different problems happening all the time – kidney infections, lung infections, the organs started to close down. On 4 October 1959, I saw the ambulance pass me while I was walking home from Mass along Two Wells Road. I saw it stop at our house again. I ran home and Dad was being treated and I was told that he was going to hospital again, this time to the new Lyell McEwan Hospital in Elizabeth. Something else had collapsed.

There were a lot of people at the house, I don't know where they came from or who they were. All I remember was Dad being carried out through the kitchen on a stretcher, and he stopped the ambulance men from walking. I was standing in the corner crying and I looked at Dad and all I could see in his eyes was lots of love and pain. We were never a family that spoke of loving one another, but I could see it in his eyes; he was telling me that he loved me. He knew it was the end and he died in the ambulance, not getting to the hospital. Mum went with him of course. I think Terry followed in his car. Dad was only 48 years old. It is terrible watching someone you love slowly getting thinner and thinner, until they don't look like the person you knew a few months earlier.

I was taken to a friend's house and later Father Abfalter came and told me that Dad had died. I don't remember who took me home later but Mum was sedated – she had a nervous breakdown. Terry's fiancée was at the house and we slept on the lounge floor outside Mum's room. Next morning Dad was buried at Salisbury. I was not allowed to go; I had to look after Mum. Apparently it was a big funeral with nearly all the Commonwealth cars and drivers there. Terry was his usual rock, not saying anything, but screaming inside. He really missed Dad. We did not realise until then that Dad had lost so much weight (he was about 17/18 stone and went down to 5/6 stone) but we realised that Terry and Dad looked like each other. Terry used to shave Dad every day before he went to work and he was worried sick about Mum.

Mum and I were still paying hospital bills two years after Dad died. We were a bit resentful about that because they had been unable to fix him up again.

On my wedding day, I really, really missed him. Terry gave me away, that was lovely, but it would have been great to have Dad. I still miss him every single day, not a day goes by when I don't talk to him, and I always feel him beside me when I'm driving.

It came out in later years that Dad might have died from the effects of the radiation he received at Maralinga. Being a driver, he was surrounded by radiation; they transported all the different equipment around the place, setting up equipment ranging from cars, buildings and heavy transport trucks. They checked everything afterwards to see the effects of the bomb. Some equipment was destroyed but some wasn't touched. But the equipment had to be driven away and checked. I assume that the vehicles were radioactive.

Terry was in the offices but when a bomb was going off they were told to go outside and stand facing away from the bomb blast with their hands over their eyes. They were seeing 'history'. Terry always said it was like looking at an X-ray; he could see every bone in his hands. Terry kept quiet about being at Maralinga. I don't know whether he knew more because he worked in the offices, or because he was there longer and he put two and two together. Seeing all the UK scientists working with protective gear on, he realised it was a dangerous place. He never told his wife and family, and the stress of that must have been terrible. He had to go for tests at the hospital because he was having pains in his chest. It turned out he had thyroid problems and also heart problems. That has never happened before in our family – except for me. He was on the medication warfarin, which his wife found in his pocket after he had died. He was only 58 when he had a massive heart attack.

I can't remember the exact year but when I was in my late thirties I found a lump on my neck. I felt very tired and couldn't keep up with the rest of the family like I used to. The doctors kept saying it was my hormones and my age. At last one doctor listened to me and said: 'I think it is your thyroid gland – it is under-active.' So after tests I had the lump and my thyroid gland removed because it was not known if it was malignant or benign until it was removed. Thank God it was benign. But I have had a lot of health problems since then. I am now on medication for the rest of my life. I discovered that in October 1956, the wind carried the radioactive cloud from Maralinga over Adelaide. I wonder what effect that might have had.

In 1970, when our daughter was born, my mother was diagnosed with cancer of the womb. She had a terrible time and was strapped to the bed and had Cobalt treatment. Luckily she got over it but had terrible effects for the rest of her life with her hair going orange, nails coming out, and terrible diarrhoea every couple of weeks. To this day I put her illness down to the effects of Maralinga, either the dust that was blown down, or washing Dad and Terry's clothes, which we are sure would have been full of radioactive dust.

So, Maralinga has badly affected our whole family. Terry married after being at Maralinga and his eldest daughter has thyroid problems, his youngest daughter was always a sick child with one thing or another, rashes, allergies and other illnesses. She had to give up her netball that she loved and also gave up work. Last year she was on dialysis for eight months before she had a kidney transplant. She has a nine-year-old son and when she wanted to have a child, the doctors told her it would be very dangerous with her past record of health, but she was determined, and luckily everything was alright. She has her father's same determination in life. But of course she has to be on medication for the rest of her life because of her kidney transplant.

Looking back now, I realise that the men who were sent to Maralinga were treated as if they were of no consequence (they had good pay). The British and Australian governments knew what was going on but they have not accepted any responsibility.

Joseph Baker

My friend Harry Frost and myself were in National Service together, and both of us applied to the Department of Works to work at Maralinga. After travelling for two days on the train, we arrived at the Watson railway siding, which was aptly named 'The Tea and Sugar Train' because it carried supplies to the outback. We were taken to the township of Maralinga where at a group meeting it was explained that we would be in contact with radioactivity. No harmful effects were explained to us, and the best thing to do was to take long showers daily after work and we should be alright.

I was a truck driver and plant operator and I worked on making roads and bomb sites. I remember areas being fenced off with a single strand of wire with white paper attached and being told not to enter these areas as they were radioactive. Perhaps the strand of wire was meant to protect us! I used to drive to one of the test explosion sites where the earth had turned to glass, and all the trucks, planes, and houses that they placed there to observe the effect of the explosions were still in place.

I carried limestone onto the new roads and sites. The dust was so thick that visibility was down to ten to 20 yards. We had no respirators, only goggles, and a damp cloth over our nose and mouth. Our fore-man, Hughie Maurer, tried to keep the dust down with water tankers but to no avail. I worked these machines the whole time I was at Maralinga; it was hard and dirty work. Also, there were a lot of Irish and Germans who had just finished working on the Snowy Mountain Scheme. British Army camp 'Roadside' was mainly for young British National Servicemen. I have often wondered how they got on in later years. They had no wire to protect them! When I finished I was flown back to the Edinburgh airfield and I can remember kissing the tarmac. All this happened when I was only 21.

When I returned to Adelaide it was discovered that I had lesions on my left lung. I remember doctors being very interested and discussing the links between my condition and radioactivity. The doctors removed the upper lobe of my left lung. I have tried to access the records of my operation, but they are missing, the only records I can find are my admittance and discharge papers to the Royal Adelaide Hospital.

I later met and married my wife. Unfortunately she has had three miscarriages and I have often wondered if it was my involvement at Maralinga that caused them.

Gary Ryan

Gary was given the job of laying footpaths around the administration quarters at Maralinga Village. This area was off limits to anyone except for working parties.

His main job was as a truck driver. After a couple of weeks of concreting, Gary was given a truck and used it to transport a gang of labourers out of the camp to do things such as move rocks which had been blown over by the blast of one of the atomic bomb tests.

The drivers were allotted shared tents for living quarters. Meals were served in the canteen and salt tablets were handed out as you entered the canteen because of the heat. It was also rumoured that bromide was in the food!

His supervisor took him out to see some of the trucks that were scattered around the bomb test site. They were placed there to see how they were affected by the blast. He was also told that the vehicles had to be decontaminated before they could be put back into service. When the steam cleaner did not work they were just given a hot wash.

One day he was told to assemble on the airstrip, and was told that a small atomic bomb was to be exploded about 20 miles away. They all had to face the other way, as it could damage their eyes, and they were informed that they would be told when it was safe to turn around. When they did turn around they saw the mushroom cloud. Not knowing the danger, they were quite excited to see such a big part of Australia's history.

Gary has suffered various medical problems such as vascula polyps, prostate operation and epileptic fits. When he asks doctors if it is anything to do with his work at Maralinga or Woomera, the doctors say 'they cannot tell'. It shows how naive everyone was then, and perhaps now. The lack of information given to workers going into this dangerous place is a shocking indictment of the authorities. The men were covered in dust most of the time. The question that has not been answered is: 'Did the dust contain wind-blown radioactive particles from the tests?'

Fallout for a journalist by Peter W Harvey

The first news of probable fallout and radioactive contamination from the Maralinga atom bomb tests affecting a wide area centred on Hamilton Downs Station, and published in the *News* on 6 October 1956, resulted in the end of my career as a journalist.

On that Saturday morning I was, as usual, starting around four in the morning as cables editor for the *News* and radio news journalist for 5DN (a commercial radio station in Adelaide) providing the morning news bulletins.

My day usually ended around 11 am, and being a Saturday most of the general writing staff were off duty and only the sports writers were around in any strength. This meant that between the Chief of Staff or his alternate and myself, we took most outside calls and news service calls.

On this day I was near to completing my tasks when we had a call from H C Davis, owner of Hamilton Downs Station in the far north. I took the call. He told me of his concerns about the effects of fallout from the Maralinga tests, saying that sheep and cattle had been affected over his country north-west of Alice Springs.

He said that other landowners in the area had also reported serious problems with their stock and he felt the problem had to be made public.

Rohan Rivett (editor) and other senior executives of the paper were not available so the acting Chief of Staff and I took the decision to publish immediately in order to put the problem in the public arena. I wrote the article. The publication of this story set the problem squarely with the authorities to defend.

Their reaction was delayed until the following Tuesday, the day Parliament returned, when the Minister of Supply, Howard Beale, took a 'Dorothy Dixer' question in Parliament from a Country Party member about the report. Beale's response was that there was no radioactive contamination.

The authorities certainly 'nobbled' the originator of the story and set the dogs on the *News*. Rebuttals then came from government sources and were published in both the *News* and the *Advertiser*.

For me it was the second time the defence forces had reacted to my writings. The first was as a former Duntroon cadet, when I blew the whistle on the outrageous initiation and bastardisation that occurred at the Royal Military College. This syndicated story resulted in personal abuse as well as attempts to reach me through management.

The two events proved a bit much for some in the *News*, and I added to their woes when, as a feature writer, I developed a series on the treatment of Aborigines and likened their circumstances to apartheid in South Africa.

This meant that I left the *News* and became a freelance writer until April 1957, when I started a whole new career in the Northern Territory Administration. This turned out to be a major turning point in my career, becoming a staffer to Cabinet ministers, corporate relations executive in a major US Corporation, consultant and both university teaching and Research Fellowships in communication. The story and my treatment probably did me a favour – I wish I could say the same about the truths of the Maralinga atomic bomb tests.

Brian Potter

My full name is Brian John Potter, born July 1925, in South Australia. I was working for the CSIRO in 1956, when I was asked if I would be interested in going to Maralinga to work with a biological team.

I was at Maralinga for approximately two months somewhere between August and October 1956. I was there for three Buffalo tests, only working during the first two tests. I witnessed the third but left soon after. Our duties consisted of determining the effects of fission products (radioactive debris from the atomic explosions) on animals and pastures. The animals mainly consisted of sheep and goats. They were placed in the forward area behind dirt mounds to ascertain the effects of fallout on their skin, hair, etc. We also put [boxes of] grasses in the fallout area and this was later fed to animals to do further tests.

From time to time we required the assistance of drivers to transport carcasses to be buried in pits and to help in laboratories. These drivers were, I think, not required to go into the forward area.

I am concerned when I hear stories of people being allowed to wander around without protective clothing and there being no security.

We were very strict about our safety precautions. There was a dirty (radioactive) area barrier and we always wore protective clothing and had our monitors on while in this area. Before returning to the clean areas we showered and were monitored. If there was any reading we were sent back to shower again until we got the all clear. We then stepped back over the barrier and dressed into our street clothes.

I carried a dosimeter and a badge when I was working in dirty areas. I think the monitoring devices were checked daily. When not working in the dirty areas these were only checked weekly.

I believe that the security to enter the forward area was very strict. I can't say that it would have been easy to bypass the Health Physics caravan although there was foliage around the caravan and I guess it could have been possible if someone was foolish enough. I did not go into the forward area after the blast to collect the animals. Two of our group, Major (Dr) Hardy and Major (Dr) Crook were responsible for this task after each blast.

I viewed the three Buffalo blasts with a group of other scientists;

we were about 12 miles from ground zero. I didn't have any blood tests before or while at Maralinga. From what I can remember blood tests only seemed to be given to persons who received a high dose rate.

The detonation of the bombs seemed to be a bit of a shambles, with firing being delayed several times because of the weather and conditions. At one stage I had to go up in a chopper to retrieve a goat that had broken loose and was wandering around. There were a lot of choppers up at the same time searching for Aboriginals, who were reported to be in the area. However, no sign of any Aboriginals was found and eventually the firing went ahead.

Document signed by Brian J Potter,
witnessed by R J Whittle,
Justice of the Peace, 12 February 1988.
Supplied by Enid Potter and Patricia Donnelly.

Mr Potter was diagnosed with various skin lesions in 1972 and cancer in 1993. He died in February 1995.

In 1955, one year before the Maralinga tests began, an Aboriginal family of the Maralinga-Tjarutja people, the Milpuddies, set off from the Everard Ranges for Ooldea, not knowing that their people had been moved to Yalata close to the coast. They followed the old rock waterhole route and used the newly formed dirt tracks where they could. Eventually they came to Maralinga and perhaps they passed by one of the signs saying: 'WARNING. You are approaching a RADIOACTIVE AREA'–although naturally Eddie Milpuddie, the young wife, would not have been able to read the signs.

The second 1956 bomb was a ground burst of 1.5 kilotons on 4 October at the Marcoo site. It left a large crater. On 14 May 1957, Eddie, her husband and children were camping in the crater or on the edge or it. She tells how soldiers came and took her and her family to the Maralinga Village. It was a shocking trip in the vehicle; they had never ridden before and they vomited everywhere. At Maralinga they were given the first showers of their lives, with soap that got into their eyes and blinded them. It was a frightening experience, made worse for Eddie by the fact that initially she thought there was another woman in the shower with her – until she realised there was a mirror and she was alone. (The 'lubra cried', reported The Royal Commission.) They were showered four or five times before the Geiger counter showed an acceptable level of radioactivity. They were then given clothes. The soldiers shot their four hunting dogs.

No medical follow-up ever occurred. Eddie was pregnant at the time of the incident and she subsequently buried a stillborn baby (she believed it was because of poison in the ground). Her next baby died, aged two, of a brain tumour in 1963 and the next was born very premature.

The Milpuddie incident was considered extremely serious for the AWTSC (it was not recorded in the minutes of the Committee). After all, it exposed the flaws in the security at the Maralinga site. Colonel Durance, Range Commander, also viewed the incident in the light of its possible political ramifications, and the Native Patrol Officer, Walter MacDougall (mentioned in Chapter 3) helped cover it up by meeting the Milpuddies and telling them that 'they had accidentally seen something of a whiteman's ceremony, they should not declare anything to other white men'. Durance was later to tell the Royal Commission that this incident (called the Pom Pom incident) caused a fuss in government and military circles and could have led to the cancellation of the tests. As the Royal Commission observed, hushing up the affair was one thing; doing nothing about it was another. The health of the surviving members of the Milpuddie family was not monitored until after 1980.

This type of negligence is not uncommon in the stories of this chapter. The Australian government has, on several occasions, told Peter Webb that he was never at Maralinga. Until, that is, he showed them the entry for his time at Maralinga on his service record. Mrs Potter has been in touch with various authorities in Canberra and South Australia. But after the initial acknowledgement of her letters no one has ever been back in contact with her.

The bombs were exploded on 14 September: 0.9 kilotons fired at 2.35 pm; 25 September: 5.67 kilotons fired at 10.00am; 9 October: 26.6 kilotons fired at 4.15 pm

By 1957, one would have expected the Health Physics 'boffins' at Maralinga to take a more cautious approach to the risks of radiation-induced diseases. The world's greatest scientists were receiving more and more media attention, warning the world's population of the dire consequences of the atmospheric testing of nuclear weapons. They issued a blunt warning during the year, effectively saying 'stop it now or expect an enormous increase in deadly cancers.' This campaign led to a partial test-ban treaty but this was far too late for Maralinga.

John Bradley tells us about the lack of care taken to mini-mise the risks of exposure to radiation. Ian McKiggan, along with Doug Rickard, was a part of the Radiological Detection Unit (RDU), Department of Defence (see Chapter 7 for Doug's account). Mara Marchioro gives us an account of her father, who worked at Maralinga as a construction hand. Her father, Drago Anicic, seems to have had all the hallmarks of radiation sickness. Vera Edwards lost her brother, Robert Schmidt, to cancer after he worked at Maralinga.

John Bradley
The RAAF send me to Maralinga

I enlisted in the RAAF early in 1947 and was posted to Maralinga in December 1956. I was a motor mechanic and worked in the motor vehicle workshop servicing vehicles. The vehicles were those used on the site and they often had to be steam-cleaned before they could be repaired. (If any one has seen this job they will know that mud tends to fly everywhere.) Two diesel trucks were left in the 'hot' area for the large 'Taranaki' bomb on 9 October 1957.

How I witnessed the bomb

The Taranaki bomb was exploded in the air, being held up by two large balloons. We were ordered to a spot eight to ten miles from the bomb test site to witness the explosion. There were also visitors and newspaper people there. We had to face away from the blast to protect our eyesight from the blinding flash. We felt the heat of the blast on the back of our necks. After three seconds we were ordered to turn 'round and face the bomb. What we saw was amazing and frightening. There was a shimmering light and gradually a cloud rose up, after expanding and then sucking up material. I think there were streaks of light (from tracer rockets) but I can't be sure as it was 46 years ago. The mushroom cloud gradually started to drift away. Approximately twenty minutes after the blast I led a convoy of trucks, caravans and water tankers to about 100 yards from ground zero. I was the closest to the actual epicentre of the blast.

As you drove towards the test site you could see the devastation of the natural vegetation; there were fires burning and the ground was very hot and dusty. I had to scratch a hole in the dirt with my hands to level the legs of a caravan that I was setting up. I also threw dirt over burning sleepers to put out the fires; they were laid down to mark where we were to park our vehicles. While doing this I was amazed to see a bloke walking over a rise towards us. I think he was observing the test from one of the bunkers.

One of the scientists ran a Geiger counter over me and said I was way over the safety limit and that I had to leave the area, but I was unable to do so until I had finished setting up the caravan. We also had film badges on, which we handed in, but we were never told the results. What was my radiation dose? I remember sitting in my truck and eating an apple only one hundred yards from the epicentre.

John Bradley

My health problems

Before I left Maralinga I had to seek medical treatment for my feet, which swelled up and commenced oozing thick yellow pus between my toes. Later, on being posted back to Laverton in Victoria in 1958, I was admitted to the RAAF hospital there with the same problem. The doctors gave me no explanation and they treated me with penicillin. I remember a medical orderly saying he had never seen anything like it. I am convinced that these problems were due to radiation damage. I left the RAAF in December 1960 and I had bouts of vomiting and I was also anaemic – this lasted for 20 years. I am convinced that I suffered from radiation sickness.

What it was like to be a guinea pig

We were not given any instructions regarding safety precautions, nor issued with protective clothing. We wore our summer uniforms. The scientists were dressed in spaceman-type outfits and had showers equipped to clean off any radioactive dust. I consider that we were treated as guinea pigs at Maralinga; we were in a zone as dangerous as any war zone.

Ian McKiggan
From navy to civilian technician

On Monday 24 July 1957 I commenced my career as a technical assistant. For Operation Antler, a team of civilians was to operate the Australian RDU (Radiation Detection Unit). It was this new unit (replacing the service personnel) I had applied to join and on 24 June we assembled in the Melbourne headquarters. Doug Rickard arrived from Queensland the next day.

We were an extraordinarily diverse lot. For the next fortnight or so, we attended daily classes at the Commonwealth X-ray Laboratories, which had an office in La Trobe Street, Melbourne. We now comprised the RDU, and proceeded to Adelaide, to the WRE at Salisbury. From there we drove to our base camp at Mt Clarence, about 45 kilometres west of Coober Pedy. I had been taught with one of the other members of the group (Bob Peagam) how to remove the thyroids from sheep. Thyroids, of course, are very fond of iodine, and iodine-131 (radioactive iodine) is produced in the atomic bomb. Since sheep eat saltbush and spinifex, and these bushes would collect the fallout, the considerable numbers of animals in our area would be a direct source of data about the levels of radioactivity and the passage of the radioactive cloud or plume. The Department had previously written to the pastoralists of the region, advising them of the requirement and guaranteeing a price of five pounds per sheep.

During September and October we were on the road a lot, gathering sticky film badges, collecting sheep thyroids and reporting background dose rates.

The first Antler round was called 'Tadje', which was mounted on an aluminium tower 100 feet (31 m) high. It was detonated at 1435 hours (2.35 pm) local time on Saturday 14 September. Tadje gave the very low yield of 1.5 kilotons. We saw no sign of the blast at Mt Clarence. However, for reasons which the British kept top secret for over two decades, this bomb was far more deadly than its relatively low power would have suggested.

Because of errors in predicting the likely wind direction, our teams were many miles away from the fallout plume, and no 'hot' dust was collected. However, later that night we came across the 'pay dirt', using our hand-held monitors. It was fairly low-level stuff, as might be expected from such a little 'feller'.

The second round was called 'Biak' and was also tower-mounted. It was detonated at 1000 hours (10 am) local time on Wednesday 25 September, and yielded about six kilotons. As with the first bomb, we listened over the radio to the countdown and were rewarded with the sight of a flash in the western sky. It was too far away to hear, however.

This time our teams were better located (on the Alice Springs road), and were well-sited to collect the fallout dust when it arrived about eight hours later. Doug Rickard's team happened to be right under the hottest part, and he got so much in his hair – which was long, lank and well-Brylcreemed – that it had to be cut off when he got back to camp. There was no way the 'crap' would wash out!

The third round was called 'Taranaki' ... Taranaki was suspended from balloons 1000 feet (310 m) above the ground, and was the most powerful of the series, at 27 kilotons. It was detonated at 1615 hours (4.15 pm) local time, on Wednesday 9 October 1957. It was the only bomb actually seen by my team, from our location on the Maralinga–Emu road. The flash was rather like a distant lightening strike, but being just over the horizon, there was no danger to our eyes or ears. By the time the fireball came into view, it was cherry red, soon expanding and rolling into a vast mushroom cloud. It was awesome in its majesty. It passed us well to the south but was several kilometres across by the time it approached the Alice road. We found out later that fallout occurred over most of the eastern half of Australia although not too hot – it was a relatively 'clean' bomb or its size. Adelaide, Melbourne and Sydney all copped some. Taranaki was the last nuclear device exploded in Australia.

Back at Mt Clarence the teams broke up in October, and I found myself in the third group with temporary positions at Salisbury – with rotation to Maralinga in six months.

———

Chapter Thirteen of Ian's memoir is entitled 'The Enemy Within' and describes his battle with cancer in 1990, after he had experienced an increasing paralysis.

———

There was a walnut-size piece of bone growing into the spinal cavity in the second-from-the-bottom rib vertebra. This had crushed the spinal cord into a quarter of its normal space, and it explained the paralysis.

It was a very happy Ian who woke up (after surgery) ... I could see the sunshine on the clouds outside the window. That meant I was still alive. I could also wiggle my toes ... But I wasn't out of the woods yet ... I had a long talk with the oncologist ...

Drago (Joe) Anicic by Mara Marchioro
How my dad became involved in Maralinga

My father was involved with the handling of chemicals at the WRE, Department of Supply. In 1955 he was asked if he wanted to work at Maralinga to earn what they called 'good money' at Maralinga. He asked what sort of duties he needed to perform and they said 'anything'. His duties ranged from groundkeeping, housekeeping and cleaning. My mother told me that he changed during 1956 and became quite distant while on leave at home.

He would be away between six to eight weeks at a time and then come home for one to two weeks. Mother would question Dad on numerous occasions about Maralinga but he told her he couldn't say anything as he was sworn to secrecy. Finally, Mum's persistence paid off and he told her how they used to make up dummy towns, put mannequins in old buildings before explosions, just to see the after-effects of the explosions. He was also asked to drive trucks and carry waste to their destinations. He was supplied with what they said was protective clothing.

In early 1957 my father was required to participate in a witness programme, being assured that no harm would come to him. In this way he became one of the indoctrinees. He was given a pair of sunglasses, told to stand in line with many other participants, have his back turned to an explosion and then turn around and witness the bomb cloud afterwards. One of the tests was at the Biak location, Maralinga, on 25 September. Due to this test he was not allowed leave to come home and visit my mother in hospital where she gave birth to me on 29 September.

Dad's health problems

During the time he worked at Maralinga he started to have health problems with his skin. The palms of his hands would split open and bleed. He went to the Maralinga Hospital and the doctor ordered a special cream from England for him. He also had to wash his hair with a special dye as he was having problems with his scalp and his hair was falling out. He didn't finish work at Maralinga but came home and got a job as a taxi driver. After a few months he was contacted and asked if he wanted to be part of a clean-up crew at Maralinga. He refused, as he was quite happy doing what he was doing. In 1962 he was told he had to go back to Maralinga as part of a skeleton crew to help bury waste. He participated and finally came home for good in 1964.

He had numerous jobs afterwards, mainly on building sites. He seemed to be getting over his problems but in 1974 he really started to get sick. He would get up in the morning, have breakfast and then go outside and vomit fiercely. He would have to pull off the road while driving due to dizzy spells. He went to the doctor, who diagnosed him with stomach ulcers and gave him medication. He complained daily with constant headaches and cramp in both legs. The headaches turned to migraines. He would lay on the lounge at night with his head cradled in his hands, screaming with pain, saying all he saw

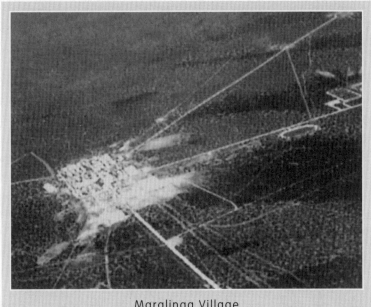
Maralinga Village

when he closed his eyes were flashes of lightning. He would walk around the kitchen table all hours of the morning to try to relieve the pain in his legs.

His condition worsened and he was sent to the Royal Adelaide Hospital for X-rays and was told that they couldn't find anything wrong but needed to be operated on to remove the ulcers. He was opened up from above the rib cage to abdomen and stitched up again. He was full of cancer. His pathology report dated 28 August 1975 states Metastatic undifferentiated malignant tumour, Lymph nodes, Malignant Tumour, Liver most likely as Reticulum Cell Sarcoma. Lymphosarcoma (Hodgkin's Disease, Leukaemia) Reticulum; retinitis, disease of the eyes, caused by excessive exposure to light. Sarcoma; Malignant cancerous tumour.

He then started a course of treatment from his specialist and by early 1976 went into remission. He was frail, thin and by this time he had lost all of his hair. He'd lost his pride and dignity, was depressed and went through excessive mood swings. He then decided to go to the gym and slowly try and build up his strength again. He finally got a note saying he could go back to work on light duties. Things were starting to look better.

On 24 June 1976, my mother received a phone call from the Royal Adelaide Hospital. My father had been brought in due to a work related accident. He had fallen from a building he was working on (light duties!) Whether or not he passed out or slipped, we will never know. He passed away at approximately 10.30 pm that same evening. They said the cause of death was a massive brain haemorrhage. His death certificate states that he died of a malignant tumour of the liver and brain haemorrhage.

As far as I am concerned, the Australian and British governments used, abused, and ill-treated him. They contributed towards the suffering and deaths of thousands of ex-servicemen, military personnel, civilians and Aborigines during the atomic testing due to the lies they told. All I can do is cross my fingers, hope and pray that my daughter and/or her children do not inherit any complications due to genetic problems from her grandfather! This was a disaster that befell an ordinary family. It should never have happened.

Robert Schmidt by Vera Edwards

I am writing about what happened to my brother, who died in 1990 at the age of 59 years. The 'Shell Company' sent him up to Maralinga where he stayed for approximately six years.

We noticed that after the bomb blast, when my brother came home on leave, he always complained about his stomach and asked my mother to just make plain meals like stew, roast lamb, etc. Every time he came it got worse, and the doctors couldn't find out what was wrong. They thought that as he was a smoker, that was the problem, but with his job at Shell he was around petrol all the time and could not smoke anyway, so he could not be considered a heavy smoker.

When he eventually came home his hand was crippled up. Shell Company wanted to know if we had any hereditary crippling hand problems in the past. My mother told them: 'There wasn't any deficiency in our family.' So Shell paid for the operation to repair his hand. He couldn't open it fully and he was working in the office. When one of the drivers went on leave or was sick, Bob would have to handle the drums, which obviously had fallout on them.

Later on he had to have cataracts taken off both eyes, the Company again paid for the operation. Finally he died of a massive heart attack. There is no record of heart problems in our family.

We know that Bob was at Maralinga for the bomb tests and we have photographs that men took when the bomb went off. Bob also told me that English military personnel, colonels, majors etc. had died before him.

I had to ring the Shell Company in Melbourne after he died as he had retired and was receiving his superannuation monthly payments. When I told them he had died and I thought it was due to him working at Maralinga when the bomb went off, the man at the other end just hung up the phone!

R W Elborough

I worked at Maralinga Village for eight months in 1957 during the 'Antler' test series with the P M G Department (now Telstra).

My health is not good and my three sons also have health problems. My first son was born with severe dermatitis. This meant that he couldn't wear any clothes. He had very limited vision and only 90 per cent hearing in one ear. His vertebras were wedge-shaped and he had deformed bones in his feet. My second son developed a blood problem, which resulted in epilepsy when he was two or three days old. My third son was born with one leg longer than the other. Because of this he can't run or play sport.

I have been corresponding with the Department of Supply (now Primary Industries and Energy) and Veterans' Affairs for many years with no result. The Commonwealth government is in a state of 'total denial' about their responsibilities.

Professor E W Titterton, the government's advisor for many years, was our worst enemy. He would swear that black was white without batting an eye. However, I suspect that Australian civilians will all be long gone before our Australian government accepts any health cause, or link, or liability over what the men suffered because of the tests.

It is my three sons that I feel badly for; I did not know that being at Maralinga would create their problems.

———

It is hard to believe that the military authorities could be so callous and cavalier with men's health. In planning for a battle, the military takes the possible casualties into account. Not so here. There was no 'battle plan'.

These civilian accounts are just few of many, and while there are service records that we could refer to in the quest for compensation for military personnel, the number of civilians that were affected will never be known.

7 – Deception and Ignorance

The story of an Aussie bloke and the element cobalt

Doug Rickard is one of Australia's true heroes. His survival for so long was what some might call a miracle. The events described here cannot be brushed aside as being the responsibility of the Safety Committee. One seemly insignificant decision was to have such tragic consequences. Ian McKiggan also met up with Doug as a member of the Australian Health Physics Team (AHPT) in April 1958. They were at Mount Clarence together, but in different teams.

Cobalt is quite harmless in its normal form (normal non-radioactive isotope). Indeed, it is the essential constituent of vitamin B12. However, in another form (another isotope), it is deadly. How it came to be used in the atomic bomb programme is yet another fascinating, or should we say deceitful, part of the story of the nuclear weapons' tests on Australian soil.

Doug Rickard
Getting a job

One Monday morning I rang the Commonwealth Department of Supply (D of S) about a job I had applied for. They were looking for Technical Assistants and Technical Officers. An understanding of electronics was advantageous, but what was interesting was that the job involved 'a period at a remote location' and later on transfer to the D of S offices at Salisbury near Adelaide. They explained that it was necessary for me to go to Melbourne for two weeks training, but they still refrained from saying where the 'remote location' was situated. The other 15 people had already turned up in Melbourne and were in the process of having their security clearances and other paperwork completed. I arrived there late Monday and proceeded to the hotel where the D of S had reserved accommodation for the whole group. That evening I met several members of the group and they explained that they had spent all day doing paperwork, but were still no wiser as to the 'remote location'.

On Tuesday morning I had to proceed to the ASIO Offices where I had to sign various security documents, and by lunchtime I was told to report to the Commonwealth X-ray and Radium Laboratories (CXRL) where the training was being given. The training started out on the theory of nuclear physics and suddenly things started to become clear. There had been some reports in the papers for several months about the possibility of further British atomic weapons tests in Australia, and that was where we were going. Maralinga. The excitement was palpable. At last we knew where we were going. The atomic weapons test project was establishing a field site some distance from Maralinga at the Mount Clarence sheep and cattle station. Coober Pedy was also on Mount Clarence property, but Mount Clarence was so large that Coober Pedy was still over a half-hour drive away. We were to go to the Mount Clarence camp and from there we were to follow the fallout from the atomic weapons as it travelled over the countryside.

As well as training in nuclear physics, we were taught how to operate a number of radiation measuring instruments, and were introduced to basic decontamination procedures. The training was interesting as nuclear physics was a totally new field for all of us, but the two weeks of training was soon up and we were to proceed to Mount Clarence.

Measuring the radioactivity in the atomic bomb clouds

On the Monday morning most of us flew to Adelaide, however three of our team were absent. They had been kept back for one day's additional training. This training turned out to be the procedures necessary to remove the thyroid glands from sheep. The rest of us were transported to the RAAF base at Edinburgh north of Adelaide. From there we were taken to a Mount Clarence camp in a RAAF Bristol Freighter.

After a couple of days the group became properly organised. We were divided up into four teams. One of the senior members of the group, Neal Tindall, was appointed group leader and would remain at the base camp at Mount Clarence to act as overall control. The remaining people were divided up into teams to man the four survey vehicles. Three of the vehicles had a four-man team. Although I was the youngest member of the group, I was made team leader of the fourth vehicle, but there were only three of us to man it. My team had been made up of the rag tag and bobtail of the whole group; the other two members of my team were the oldest members of the group.

Shortly after our arrival at Mount Clarence there occurred an incident that had us all mystified. It was still early days yet and we were still getting to know one another. But in the middle of the night when most of us were still asleep a black car arrived. There were some hurried discussions ending up with one of our number being escorted to the black car and they disappeared in the night. We never did find out what the whole incident was about.

We were finally ready for action. All preparations at Maralinga had been completed and now everything depended on the weather. It was important that the wind was blowing from the south-east round to the south-west. This was to ensure that the fallout did not go over large population sites like Adelaide. Meteorologists from Giles in Western Australia, Alice Springs, and at Maralinga itself would provide weather data to the scientists so that they could determine if the conditions would be correct for a test firing. Generally it was preferable to fire the weapon around sunrise when the wind was at its lowest. This meant that many of the people involved in the test had to get up hours before. Because of the need to allow the many staff involved to get to their places on time, it meant that the meteorologists had to make their prediction round about midnight. Of course this left several hours during which the weather could change, and change it often did.

Our group, the ARDU, often had to travel several hundred miles to arrive at our required positions in time for the blast. Each team would be given the coordinates of where they were to operate. The idea was that the teams would form a line across the line where the fallout was expected to travel. In order to arrive at our required locations in time it meant that we had to depart almost as soon as the meteorologists had decided that conditions looked suitable for a blast.

At about 1 am we would set out to our appointed locations in our Land Rovers. As soon as we arrived we would set up our radio transmitter. Later this was just a simple matter of plugging in a whip antenna, but in the beginning it meant laying out our long wire antenna, then climbing up any available tree and attaching the antenna to it. As often as not the weather would change by the time morning approached. We would get a call over our radio that the test had been cancelled due to weather conditions and we would pack up and return to Mount Clarence base camp. It was not uncommon to have two or three false tries before a blast would finally go off successfully.

When we arrived at our location our job was to do a radiation survey of our immediate vicinity using a Geiger Muller counter. This meant taking measurements at about a dozen randomly selected places. We were to take an average of these measurements and record this as the background level. Often I would find that a much higher value than the average would be found at certain locations. It soon occurred to me that these high readings were always at the base of grass clumps. The area we were working in was mainly just sandy desert with occasional traces of saltbush and desert grass. The high readings I was getting were always in the desert grass. After finding this pattern on a number of occasions I made some enquiries through the group leader Neil Tindall. The answer that came back was that fallout from the previous set of tests, the Buffalo series (in 1956), had gone in this direction. What I was finding seemed to be fallout from the Buffalo tests. The winds had blown the fine fallout material back and forth over the desert surface, and it finally accumu-lated in the base of the desert grass. I tried to point out to the people in charge that this could dramatically affect the readings we might measure, both before and after the new tests, but no one seemed interested. Still, I recorded the average background and the peak levels that I measured on our record sheet, but I got the feeling that no one was interested and they only saw my bringing up the subject as a waste of time. I was to learn that this was typical of many of the aspects of the tests and that no one was interested in anything that didn't fit in with their prior convictions.

On one occasion the fallout actually fell on us. At least we were able to get some proper radiation readings for our records. However, the consequences were more than we had expected. 1957 was the time of the bodgies and widgies (young men dressed in tight trousers and slicked-back hair and associated with wild behaviour). I was a Brylcreem boy, and used liberal amounts of Brylcreem on my hair. Anyway, when we got back to Mount Clarence camp a few passes with a Geiger counter soon showed that we were quite contaminated, so it was off to the showers. It did not take long to wash the contamination off our bodies, but I was unable to get the fallout out of my hair. Repeated washings were to no avail. In the end there was no other way but to cut off all my hair. That did the trick. After a final shave of my scalp and a washing at last the fallout was all gone. However, I have often wondered if the amount of fallout on our clothes and skin was sufficient to create problems, then just how much had we inhaled? I guess we will never know.

Anyway, our time at Mount Clarence came to a close. After just three tests in 1957, ARDU started to wind down. The Mount Clarence camp was being disassembled and the various people were returning to their normal occupations. A number of the ARDU group were offered positions at the D of S research laboratories at Salisbury, but four of us were offered positions at Maralinga. These were to be rotating positions, changing every six months. I jumped at the opportunity because I had been having such a good time at Mount Clarence. Merv Jolly was the first to go to Maralinga arriving there on 30 September 1957. I followed on 10 October.

Maralinga

At Maralinga we became part of the AHPT. The head of the AHPT was Harry Turner, the Australian Health Physics Representative (AHPR). Harry quickly introduced us to the rest of the AHPT who had been there at Maralinga during the actual tests. They were all members of the army. We were placed under the guiding hand of Sergeant Frank Smith.

Frank Smith and a number of other army personnel had formed the core of the AHPT during the tests. Now it was their turn to teach us the ropes. Initially, our duties were to man the Health Physics caravans at the test site. The caravans were the demarcation between the non-radioactive areas and the radioactive areas. There were two main caravans, one for people going into the forward area, and the other caravan was for people returning. People going into the forward area had to pass through security first. Then they would proceed to the outgoing caravan. First they would have to detail where they were going, what they were planning to do, and how long they expected to be in the area. The group leader might be issued with a map that showed the current danger spots to enable them to keep to the safe areas. Then film badges would be issued if they did not already have one and a quartz-fibre radiation dosimeter.

Why we were issued quartz-fibre dosimeters I will never know. Not only was the quartz fibre very fragile but also the charging units seldom operated correctly. Despite the fact that they were not often working we were still ordered to issue everyone going forward with a dosimeter. Many of the regular army personnel, and many of the British 'nashos' or National Servicemen, would demand a dosimeter even if we told them they were not working. Unfortunately, many somehow believed that the dosimeter (and film badges for that matter) would protect them from the effects of radiation, and we did not have the time to educate them differently.

Then they would proceed to the next part of the caravan to exchange their clothing for the white overalls that were the uniform in the forward area. A pair of grey woollen socks and white rubber boots with disposable overshoes, white cotton gloves and a head cap completed the dress. Then they would proceed to the forward area to carry out whatever tasks they had been assigned.

On their return they would enter the other caravan. Firstly, they would remove the overshoes and rubber boots, gloves, overalls, and socks. Then they would step over a small dividing partition. This partition was the line between the 'clean' and 'dirty' areas. Next was a shower, then to the radiation detectors. There was a six-foot-high machine, the 'hand-and-foot monitor'. There was a series of Geiger Muller (GM) tubes under the footplate. There were also two apertures for the hands and these too had GM tubes. This would soon indicate if there was any obvious contamination. Then one of the AHPT would run a hand-held GM instrument over the person. If at any time there was a reading above the allowed level then it was back into the showers again. When they were finally clean they could dress in their original clothing and return to the village.

While we operated the caravans, Sergeant Smith and the other members of the AHPT would be out in the forward area doing radiation surveys of the different test sites. To facilitate the surveys, radiating lines spaced at 30-degree intervals had been drawn from the ground zero point. Pegs had been driven into the ground at 100-foot intervals. Near ground zero the pegs were steel star pickets driven deep into the limestone so that only a couple of inches protruded. Further out the pegs were wooden 2' x 2' sections again driven in so that only a couple of inches protruded.

Radiation surveys were done by starting at the extreme end of one of the radiating sets of pegs. Every 100 feet at the peg a reading would be taken. The operator would pass right through ground zero and then out to the extreme of the other leg. At each point they would take a measurement and record it on a clipboard. From the end of one transit the operator would move over to the extreme end point of the next radiating line of pegs and start the process all over again.

In the beginning when radiation levels were high it was important to keep the time in the field down to a minimum. To achieve this we had a Land Rover fitted with a boom projecting from the front of the vehicle. The ionisation chamber of a measuring instrument could be fitted to the end of the boom such that it was the required one metre above the ground. A remote readout was fitted inside the vehicle. Surveys could be done quickly by driving along the lines of pegs taking readings at each peg. The problem with this system was that the readings were affected by the proximity of the Land Rover, and that often the 100-foot marker pegs were missing and it was not possible to go searching for them if the time schedule had to be maintained.

As the radiation diminished, readings started to be done manually. This had several advantages. One was that the operator could count the number of paces between pegs and be able to take readings even if the peg might be missing. Another was that just one person was required to make and record the measurement, thus minimising the number of people who were exposed to the radiation. The effect on the personnel doing the surveys was demanding. The total distance was about three and a half miles, carrying a heavy piece of equipment, and dressed from top to toe in 'protective' clothing. All this in a temperature that was often over 40 degrees in the shade! And heaven forbid that one needed to urinate during this time. It was not uncommon to arrive back at the caravans with rubber boots full to the top with a mixture of urine and sweat. It was common to lose several pounds on a single survey and so it was important to have sufficient staff to be able to rotate the people actually doing the surveys.

After a few weeks the human activity in the forward area started to decrease. As it did, the number of staff required to man the caravans also decreased and so bit-by-bit we civilians from Mount Clarence started to take over the operations from the army personnel. Smith was one of the last to go, but eventually the AHPT became just Harry Turner as AHPR, myself, Merv Jolly, Jim Davidson, and Val Krauja as technical staff, and our camp secretary. And I don't use 'camp' as in 'military camp'. While the rest of us were used to sweat and urine in 40-degree heat, Harry's male secretary was as sweet smelling as a prostitute's boudoir.

Anyway, life started to settle down to a routine of caravan duties interspersed by radiation surveys. Most of the UK personnel were gone and as the official inter-trials period was entered, most functions were taken over by Australian staff. One UK scientific staff member named Peter White was left as part of the AHP group. Peter's background was as a chemist and his function was to carry out various long-term experiments for the UK AWRE. As the UK staff who did the film badge processing had returned to the UK, Peter took over the job and I became his assistant.

Film badge processing was a relatively simple procedure. In a darkroom the film badges were disassembled and placed in a beaker of X-ray developer. The darkroom was kept at a constant temperature of 20°C so that the developing times were constant. After developing, the filmstrips were washed in tap water. Unfortunately, the cold water pipes in the Radio Biological (RB) area were all above ground and exposed to the direct sunlight. A cast iron above-ground pipe brought fresh water from the Village into a large tower mounted tank. From there, a copper pipe bought the water via an outside wall-mounted pipe to the individual taps. Because of this the temperature of the 'cold' water was often at the point where it would scald the skin. We often had problems with the high temperature water softening the emulsion of the film badges, and in extreme cases the emulsion would develop bubbles or even come off completely. Finally, the filmstrips were immersed in a beaker of fixer, washed once again, and then hung up using clothes pegs to dry. When dry, the film badges were measured on an optical densitometer. The densitometer was comprised of a power supply and low voltage light bulb. The amount of light passing through the filmstrip was measured by a photovoltaic cell connected to an analogue meter with divisions from zero to 100. There was a small piece of graph paper attached to the densitometer and it had a calibration curve drawn on it. The reading from the meter was compared with the calibration curve and this was translated into levels of absorbed radiation. The film badge holders had a strip of cadmium so that different energies of radiation could be measured. Readings were taken of the uncovered section of the film badge and the section covered by the cadmium strip. Both readings were recorded in a large notebook. Eventually Peter White had to return to the UK so I became responsible for all film badge processing and recording for the whole Maralinga staff.

There were many problems with the film badge system. First was the fact that often multiple badges were issued to the one person. This occurred because sometimes staff going into the forward area thought they had lost their film badge and another badge was issued on their re-entry to the forward area. When they finally exited the forward area both film badges were collected. It was difficult to know which badge had the correct reading so often both badge values would be entered into the log. In other cases film badges were lost completely because they were held on by just a small safety pin and often during physical labour the badge would become detached from the wearer.

In other cases the wearer would leave their film badge inside their vehicle while they were working in the forward area. The reason for this was that general day-to-day life at Maralinga could become very boring. Working in the forward area was a welcome break from the boredom of Village life, but if one had exceeded one's limit, one was restricted from access to the forward area. There was a tendency for those who knew they were approaching their radiation limit to leave their film badge in a place where it would not receive much radiation. Sergeant Smith even taught us this technique for when we too were working in the forward area. Even with this ruse there was still the times when our radiation levels were sufficiently high that we were restricted to office duties. On a number of occasions Harry Turner stopped me from doing forward duties because my radiation levels were too high. This was a great disappointment to me so when I knew my radiation levels were nearing the limit I would often leave my film badge in the glove compartment of the Land Rover. Sometimes, however, there would be just so much radiation that I wasn't able to pull this ruse and I exceeded the allowable limit, so Harry had no choice but to confine me to office duties for the remainder of the month.

Frank Smith and the last of the army had now left and our duties started to increase as we took over some of the functions from them. Somehow I ended up with some other duties as well. One of my new jobs was running the radioactive laundry. This is where all the protective clothing was washed in order to decontaminate it. There was a line of big washing machines. I would start up the boiler to raise steam, and then I would load all the clothing into the washing machines. I had to mix up a detergent and various other chemicals.

I had no idea what the different chemicals did, I was just told once by the departing army staff what to do and so I had a new job to my repertoire.

As time passed, my set of duties continued to increase. DC12 was a building in the RB area that was used for the preparation of the uranium and plutonium to be used during the so-called 'minor trials'. Because of the materials used in the hot box of DC12, there was a continuous production of thoron and other short half-life gaseous isotopes. To prevent these dangerous gases being discharged directly to the atmosphere, there was a special system to handle the exhaust gases. There was a pair of fine filters to filter out any particulate material. One or the other of these filters could be switched into circuit. It was important that these filters never became clogged so there was a water gauge measuring the pressure drop across the filters. After the filters there was a delay tank. This was a long line of joined boxes so that the time taken for the gas to pass through the delay system was enough for several half-lives to have passed and the radioactive gas decayed back to a solid particulate matter which could be filtered out.

At one stage the water gauges on the DC12 filters indicated that one of the filters desperately needed replacing and the second filter was fast approaching the same state. New filters were flown out from the UK, but no instructions or special equipment accompanied them. With my background in mechanics I saw no special difficulties in doing the actual physical work involved, but other difficulties were making themselves evident. Once the seal on the filter was breached there was the problem of contamination from the radio-active gases. Standard protective clothing and disposable gloves would provide some protection, but what to do to stop breathing in the dangerous gases? No documents covering the procedures necessary had been supplied, nor any special equipment, so we had to make up something ourselves. We did have plenty of gas masks available, and the 'yellow garage' at the RB area had several air compressors available. They were not designed for the application we had but we had no other alternatives. The gas masks really required a large volume of low-pressure air, but the compressors provided a small volume of air at a high pressure. However, my preliminary tests seemed to show that the system might work.

Peter White and I dressed in our protective clothing and donned our gas masks, but we were now out in the blazing sun and starting to do hard physical work. It soon became apparent that the air compressors were not doing the job. Soon we were gasping for breath but we already had the old filter disconnected. By this time the glass eyepieces of the gas masks were starting to fog up and obstruct my sight. I had no choice; I ripped the gas mask off and continued the installation of the new filter. As soon as the new filter was bolted into position I proceeded to wrap up the old filter in plastic to prevent any of the radioactive gases or other material from escaping. However, the damage had already been done and I had breathed in a large amount of radioactive gas.

This was not yet the end of the saga. We still had to replace the second filter. This time I took a different approach. Instead of using air compressors with their low volume high-pressure output, I needed a source of low-pressure high volume air. Soon I decided to give vacuum cleaners a try. Using the output of the vacuum cleaners we could have a source of air, all we needed was some type of hose to connect the vacuum cleaners to the gas masks. In the stores I came across some thin wall plastic tube. It was wrapped flat on a roll but when the vacuum cleaner exhaust was connected it formed a circular tube about one inch in diameter. Tests in the workshop showed that the system was capable of supplying as much air as was needed. So Peter and I set up to change the second filter. Again things started out well, but after a short while a problem started to show itself. The circular shape of the tube was only there when the tube was pressurised. It could not flex around a corner, instead it would just fold flat again and cut off all air. As I worked on the filter, the tube kept folding flat all the time. Finally, in desperation, I had to tear off the gas mask and continue to install the new filter with no protection from the radioactive gases issuing from the dirty filter.

The whole point of the above is to show how poorly we were supported from the UK AWRE at Aldermaston. Surely they were doing many filter changes. Surely they had developed all the procedures necessary to ensure the safety of the operators. And surely they would have developed the means to provide the operators with clean, uncontaminated air. We had none of that. We were just supplied with two filters and left to work out for ourselves how to do the job. This was another example of the disdain in which the UK authorities held the Australian teams.

The cobalt-60 affair

Following each explosion, the AHP group carried out nuclear radiation surveys. In the period immediately after the blasts, these surveys were carried out at very frequent intervals, but as the radiation gradually decayed, the period between the surveys increased. In order to ensure repeatability, the actual measurements were carried out at the same points each time. These measurement points were on 12 radiating lines from the ground zero point, and were spaced at 100-foot intervals along each radiating line. A wooden peg driven into the ground marked the measurement points. Generally the measurements were done by an AHP staff member walking along the radiating lines while carrying various types of instrumentation. Generally they would walk out along one line, then in along the next line, and so on. The measurements would be recorded on pre-printed forms on a clipboard.

Using the information from the radiation surveys, radiation level contour maps were drawn up by AHP staff. These maps were used as a guide to determine safe areas. However, because the measurements were only taken at the pre-marked measurements points, there were large areas within the affected area between the radiating lines where measurements were not taken.

Initially the contour lines for all blast sites were reasonably uniform. However, as time passed, and the general radiation levels began to subside as the shorter half-life elements decayed, the contour lines for the Tadje site started to show abnormalities in a northerly direction from ground zero. Initially these abnormalities were not sufficiently obvious to raise any alarms.

I did some surveys at the Tadje site about nine months after the Tadje explosion (held on 25 September 1957). Contrary to the normal practice of crossing between lines only at the extreme end of the survey line, I crossed between the survey lines at about the 700-foot point. As I traversed this previously unsurveyed area, I noticed abnormal levels of radioactivity, which attracted my interest. In particular, one of the abnormalities was that the radiation seemed to be in very discrete spots, and not evenly distributed, as normal fallout would have been.

The other abnormality was that I was using an Alpha particle measuring instrument. Normally an Alpha particle counter has to be held within one to two centimetres of the source to be measured, but I was at that time holding the sensing head at waist level as I walked along, yet I was still observing high readings!

Using my right foot (in rubber boots) I found I was able to move around the actual source of radiation, and I was able to isolate the source of radiation to about a handful of sand. A visual inspection of this small sample revealed a small (two to three millimetres) shiny, black metallic-looking pellet totally unlike any of the standard desert surface. This metallic pellet proved to be the source of the radiation.

Continuing in this way I was able to recover approximately 30 similar metallic particles which were stored in the standard specimen collection container (Dr Pat tobacco tins). It was obvious from my instruments that there were many, many more such sources, but there were far too many of them for me to collect at that time. I placed the containers in the back of the Land Rover and drove the 36 miles back to the RB laboratory area where the AHP offices were located.

When I arrived back at the laboratory area, I found that the other AHP staff were running around in some consternation as much of the laboratory instrumentation had suddenly gone haywire exactly coincidental with my arrival. A gamma-measuring instrument was obtained and a measurement of just one of the pellets showed a reading equivalent to about 30 millicuries [mC]. This confirmed that these pellets were indeed very strong gamma emitters, and the readings I had obtained on the alpha instrument has been actually due to malfunction of the instrument in such a high gamma field.

In order to ascertain the composition of the pellets, a Pierson scanning gamma spectrometer was needed, which used a sodium iodide scintillator. Just one pellet alone was so strong that the instrument was overloaded. Finally, the pellet had to be moved onto a wooden stool about 30 feet away outside the building before an accurate reading could be obtained. The characteristic double curve obtained confirmed that the material was cobalt-60 (Co60).

An attempt was made to measure the volume of one of the pellets. To do this, a calibrated pipette was about half-filled with water, and then the pellet was dropped into the pipette to measure the change in water levels. The level of radioactivity from the pellet was such that it caused blackening of the glass pipette (a phenomenon known as F-centre displacement).

Leaving Maralinga

Finally, after a few years at Maralinga I realised it was time to move on. I had exhausted the opportunities that Maralinga had to offer. When I started to talk about leaving, Garvin Hogg, one of the AWRE team who was working at DC12 on the minor trials, suggested that I might like to consider a position with AWRE at Aldermaston. It was soon apparent that AWRE were not impressed with the idea of me wandering alone around Australia with all the information about the Tadje cobalt-60 incident. This would have been a political bombshell if ever the Australian government were to find out about it, so AWRE starting making some tempting offers of a guaranteed job and accommodation in the UK. Eventually, I decided to accept their offer. Finally I left Maralinga; I flew to Adelaide, then to Melbourne where I boarded a ship bound for the UK. But that is another story . . .'

On 10 July 1958, Mr H Turner reported the facts to the AWRE: 'A number of Co60 pellets have been found in the vicinity of 700 feet North of Tadje with an average activity of 40 mC, repeat millicuries. The largest pellet (79 mC) would register 36 r/hr. The potential lethality of each pellet is increased by the fact that they are only one to two millimetres in diameter and could easily be lodged in clothing or be ingested.' (See the 1985 Royal Commission Report.)

The response to this report was an immediate and complete

security clampdown. Even though Doug was an Australian citizen working in Australia, he was taken to a British security officer who warned him very strongly not to talk about the incident to any other Australians, even his superior, Mr H Turner.

The extremely sensitive political nature of the event can be judged from an AWRE letter dated 23 July 1958: 'I mention these items to you because there is a danger that some political trouble will arise if these stories get a wide circulation.' It was evident that the Australian people, and even the Australian government, were being kept very much in the dark regarding some of the activities going on at Maralinga.

Doug had been wearing a standard issue film badge when he discovered the cobalt-60 pellets. However, when the film badge was developed it had been so saturated with radiation that it was totally black and it was impossible to determine just how much gamma radiation he had received.

The AWRE requested that the cobalt-60 be collected as soon as possible. Special lead containers were flown out from Britain for this purpose. Unfortunately, because of handling the pellets, most of the AHP staff by this time had already received the Maximum Permissible Level (MPL) allowed, so were not in a position to be able to carry out the collection process.

At that time, a number of Australian defence services personnel had arrived at Maralinga for training in radiation detection techniques. These personnel were used to collect as many of the pellets as possible. Because of the security restrictions, they were not told of the nature or danger of the material they were collecting. A number of scoops were fabricated by affixing jam tins onto long wooden handles, and the collectors used these so as to maintain a reasonable distance from the pellets. Some of the pellets were so small that they had to be collected using tweezers. Some of the personnel who had been performing the collection in this way later reported their fingers becoming red around the tips and nails.

The presence of cobalt-60 at the Tadje site had not been

reported to the AHP group, but Professor Ernest Titterton, Chairman of AWTSC, had been advised of the presence of cobalt-60 prior to the test. He chose not to pass on the information to the AHP group. When asked why, Titterton said they wanted 'to give Harry [Turner] and his workers a bit of a test.'

The Royal Commission Report (section 9.5.5) states: 'It was of great concern to the AHPR that the discovery of the cobalt-60 had been accidental.' It appears that other Australian authorities were also ignorant about the use of cobalt-60. Richardson of CXRL, the Senior Health Physics Advisor to whom Turner reported administratively, wrote to Turner on 12 August 1958: 'The discovery of the cobalt is disturbing ... We can do little about this until we receive a reply from the UK.'

It was a deliberate action by Titterton to withhold the important information regarding the presence of cobalt-60 at the Tadje explosion and this led to Doug receiving a damaging dose of deadly gamma radiation. This was, of course, criminal. No doubt Titterton was in the pocket of the British Weapons group and thought that they would get away with the use of cobalt-60.

In the nine-year period following his exposure to the cobalt-60, Doug experienced many medical problems. These included severe pain and loss of skin on his right foot (which he used to isolate the cobalt-60 pellets) and loss of skin on his right and left hands. In 1967 at the Royal Brisbane Hospital, at the age of 27, Doug was finally diagnosed with chronic myelofibrosis and myeloid metaplasia. Myelofibrosis is normally only a disease of the aged, and once diagnosed, life expectancy is normally two to three years.

Doug's account continues:

Qualifications

I had only ever reached Year 10 at school. I was so bored with what they were teaching as I already knew most of Physics, which was the subject that had taken my interest. At Maralinga, Harry Turner had been encouraging me to further my education. I finally enrolled with the South Australian School of Mines, which ran the correspondence courses in the state. When I enrolled, no special conditions were mentioned at all. The correspondence course was supposed to be two years long but I finished it in one year. Then came the time to sit for the matriculation examination in Adelaide.

I had some difficulties at this stage. Correspondence students were ineligible to sit for the matriculation examination, as they would not have been able to do the practical work. Harry Turner, Peter White, and other scientists had all signed my practical notebook confirming that, indeed, I had done the required practical work in one of the best-equipped laboratories in the state. Under these conditions the authorities decided to allow me to sit for the examination. That's where the next snag arose.

Being at a remote location meant that I would be required to sit the examination under the supervision of the State police. There were only Commonwealth police at Maralinga and the examining body was not prepared to alter their procedures for just one student. So I flew to Adelaide and sat the examination in the central examination centre.

Because of the cobalt-60 incident, I knew that there was a higher level of security in effect, but I was not prepared for the reception that I received when we landed at the RAAF airbase. As I alighted from the aircraft, two large Commonwealth policemen were there to greet me. They escorted me to a Commonwealth vehicle and drove me to the examination centre and accompanied me to my seat. The rest of the examinees were in several rows of desks at one end of the room, but my desk was way down the other end, remote from any of the other students. As I worked on the paper, the two Commonwealth police officers stood on either side of me. Heaven knows what the other students thought; perhaps they thought I was a prison inmate sitting for the examination. The examination was very simple and I finished very quickly. At the end of the exam I was again escorted back to the RAAF base and put on the aircraft for the return trip to Maralinga.

I did not think about the exam for some time, but one day I received a letter from the Adelaide University telling me that I had failed. I was flabbergasted, to say the least. The paper was so simple and was on topics that I knew well, so the last thing I was expecting was a fail. I was talking to Harry Turner about the examination and he asked me did I agree with the result. I explained how easy I had found the exam and he was very perplexed. Finally, he asked me if I had considered asking for a re-mark. I had never heard of a re-mark before, but Harry explained that if one thought one had been unfairly marked and could present a reasonable case, he could ask for a re-mark. Harry also offered to write a letter supporting my case. Finally, my examination paper was re-marked by the Professor in charge of the Physics Department at Adelaide University. Blow me down but this time I was awarded an Honours pass. It turned out that instead of using the textbooks recommended by the School of Mines, I had used all the scientific textbooks that were in the Maralinga library, and they were mainly English and American. My answers were not what the examiners were expecting so they did not understand my answers. This was just the start of my disappointments with academia.

One must wonder, based on the difficulties that Doug encountered, whether he was deliberately hindered in his studies by suspicious authorities. He had already seen too much. Perhaps the authorities did not want him to learn any more, lest he raise a case against them.

Doug's health remained reasonable until about 1980 when he started to suffer recurring bouts of severe pain in the abdomen. In 1982, this was determined by doctors at the Royal North Shore Hospital in Sydney to be due to an enlarging spleen, a characteristic of myelofibrosis. His spleen continued to enlarge over time, until in 1992 the spleen had reached a point where he was in continuous pain and the spleen itself was in danger of rupturing. His spleen was removed in 1992 at the Mater Hospital in Brisbane and weighed 1800 gm, in comparison with the approximately 100 grams of a normal spleen.

Since the removal of his spleen, Doug's liver has taken over the blood production function, and it too is now enlarging. With the loss of his spleen, his blood chemistry altered dramatically.

The platelet count rose to such a high level that in early 1993, Doug suffered two mild thromboses. He is now being treated with alpha-interferon in order to reduce the platelet count, and to help improve immunity. He is also permanently on morphine to alleviate the pains from the enlarged liver.

In 2002, at the age of 63, Doug was the longest surviving patient with myelofibrosis in the world. As such, it meant that there was no precedence or prehistory of this stage of the disease to help in its treatment. This greatly hindered the medical staff who treated him during the latter stages of his life.

There also remains the question of the long-term medical history of the Australian services personnel who were used to clean up the cobalt-60 from the Tadje site. Were follow up health studies ever conducted on them?

Doug wrote the following poignant note to us on 21 April 2002: 'I did not realise at the time just how severe that dose of radiation had been and just how detrimental it would be to my health in the long term. Now I am just waiting to die.' He died during May 2002. We acknowledge his wonderful life, his indomitable spirit to overcome such adversity, his will to live and the example he set.

Ian McKiggan
My brush with cobalt-60

I must have come close to the cobalt-60 pellets while strolling about the Tadje site. One evening I noticed my personal dosimeter was way off scale, which meant that either it was malfunctioning or I had received a hot dose. However, no one else except Doug Rickard had had a similar reading. I mentioned it to Harry Turner, who said not to worry until the film badge was developed. This took a few days. I don't recall any other oddities over the rest of the week, but one morning when I reported in at HQ, Harry Turner called me into his office. He was clearly worried and mystified. He was also more than a little suspicious that somehow I had 'cooked the books' over the level of radioactivity I had received.

Of course I hadn't 'cooked' anything and I resented the imputation.

Moreover, the high readings on both the dosimeter and the badge meant (to me), an almost certain overdose. Harry scratched his balding pate and stared at his radiation wall maps.

Then he asked me outright if I had deliberately left my dosimeter and badge near a radiation source, pointing out that there shouldn't be anything in the forward area where I had worked, nothing that would have produced the very high radiation dose so quickly. Quite frankly he didn't believe my dosimeter results, but even so, he felt compelled to pull me out of all 'yellow' area work for at least a month. In other words, I wasn't going to be much use to him for several weeks. He asked whether I had any thoughts as to how I could be gainfully employed. My answer to that was swift. As far as I was concerned, Salisbury was infinitely preferable to Maralinga. I had left a relatively prestigious position at Salisbury for an interesting but basically menial task at Maralinga. Harry liked the idea and I was sent back to Adelaide.

As it turned out, I was never to go back to Maralinga. Unknown to me, or anyone else, I retained a tiny souvenir of my time in the desert. Deep in my spine a solitary bone cell was recovering from the shock of being smashed by gamma radiation. It was to be 30 years before this cell, and its clones, made their presence felt and I fell ill.

––––––––

After Ian's brush with cancer, he decided to look-up two of his old colleagues in the RDU, to advise them about his experiences. He met Doug Rickard again around 1989. This is what he has to say about this remarkable man:

––––––––

It was good to see 'L'il Abner' (Doug's nickname at Mt Clarence) again after all those years. He was much the same in appearance and mannerisms. Sure he had a grizzled beard now, and a bit of a beer pot. (Doug assured me later that he did NOT have a beer pot. It is actually a hyper-enlarged spleen which produces this effect.) We sat around yarning for the best part of five hours, and it left me feeling sadder and wiser.

He showed me official correspondence, which states flatly that he was never exposed to more than the permitted levels of radiation. This is juxtaposed with expert medical testimony that Doug's bone marrow condition can *only* be caused by radiation exposure – and fairly massive doses at that. Doug's collection of contradictory officialese is almost surreal in its ignorance – or attempts to deceive – it's hard to tell which.

Take, for example, a letter from the WRE to Doug's employer, dated 17 February 1977. This states that the Department had no medical records pertaining to Mr Rickard between the time of his recruitment to the time of his resignation. Yet four months later (8 June 1977), the WRE personal officer was able to advise Harry Turner that these records did exist. (This correspondence is cited in Volume 2 of the Report of the Royal Commission.)

Another example is provided by the November 1983 Report: 'Health of Atomic Personnel', produced by the Commonwealth Department of Health. This is but one of numerous official position papers which states that, to the date of publication, no 'atomic' personnel had health problems linked to radiation exposure. Yet, on 31 March 1983 (nine months earlier), the Commonwealth of Australia issued a 'Determination of compensation' for Doug Rickard. This compensation pays for all Doug's medical and hospital bills for injuries sustained by exposure to ionising radiation at Maralinga!

What I couldn't understand was why the AWTSC did not put out a special warning for us to be on the alert for high-energy fission products from the Tadje site. Surely its chairman, Professor Titterton, had not been in the dark too? There was something very odd … I asked Doug what he thought. He nearly exploded. 'Do you know that Titterton had the gall to tell the Royal Commission that of course he knew that Tadje had cobalt in the works? As for not letting on, he thought it would be a worthwhile exercise for Harry Turner's boys to find the stuff.' It is perhaps a good thing that Sir Ernest Titterton is now dead – this revelation added me to the list of nuclear veterans who would have liked to kill him!

I went on to ask Doug when he first noticed clinical symptoms resulting from his exposure. He said that it was two or three years later when he was in the UK. He started getting gout-like twinges in his right foot – which was the one he used to poke around in the soil for his first cobalt pellet – followed by night sweats, and frequent intractable bouts of colds and flu. What was happening was that his bone marrow had completely packed it in – thereby destroying most of his immune defences. To cut this long and painful story short, he was eventually diagnosed with myelo-fibrosis and myelo-metaplasia. In other words, his bone marrow has turned to cardboard, and cannot produce any red blood cells. This means that the spleen must do the job, which is asking too much of it. Doug has been living on a knife-edge for quite a while, but he is made of the right stuff all right.

———

Coincidentally, Ian died about a month before Doug in 2002. They were two young men who were in the wrong place at the wrong time, who both received massive doses of gamma radiation.

8 – Maralinga: The Minor Trials 1958–1962

Assigned to the AWRE, Aldermaston, Avon Hudson was involved in the Minor Trials at Maralinga. He was sent with a team of British engineers to construct the 'Feather Beds' (the firing platforms for the Taranaki experiments). He has campaigned for recognition of the nuclear veterans and civilian personnel for over 30 years. His life has been deeply affected by a sense of injustice and callousness of successive Australian governments ignoring the plight of those caught up in 'the grand game'.

Over the years, Avon has helped many families who have been affected by the atomic bomb tests. He has a capacity to see the big picture and to provide support. As a councillor in a conservative rural district council, he has single-handendly convinced his fellow councillors that the Wakefield Regional Council should be Nuclear Free. His account of his time at Maralinga is an edited version of his deposition to the Royal Commission into the British Nuclear Tests in Australia in 1985.

Following Avon's story is an account from Mike Robinson, who was coerced into going to Maralinga by the WRE at Salisbury. George Stirna was also at Maralinga Village during the tests – even this relatively remote area was not safe. Edwin Bailey moved to Aldermaston in 1953 and began working on Britain's nuclear weapons programme at AWRE. He died on 30 January 2003.

Avon Hudson

In 1956 I joined the RAAF and my experience with Maralinga started in 1960 after I had returned from Darwin. I had been at Laverton for a few weeks and was assigned to the Air Movements' section. For the first time for quite a while I was quite content and happy with what I was doing.

One morning I was summoned to the section officer's office where I talked with a couple of civilian gentlemen They asked me a lot of questions about my life. I asked them what it was all about and they said it had nothing to do with me, I was there to answer questions. They continued asking me questions, about my family, my sisters, brothers, uncles and cousins and goodness knows what else. They wanted to know a lot about our family's history. In the end they said they would be in contact and left.

When I was posted to Maralinga I realised the reason for the security check. In a few days I was off to Maralinga. I knew quite a lot of people who had been to Maralinga and being an inquisitive bloke I knew quite a bit of what had gone on up there. But nothing prepared me for what I saw on arrival. I was astounded to find that it was a hive of activity. Everything was abuzz with military ser-vicemen from the UK and Australia. There would have been about one-hundred-odd technicians and scientists – we called them boffins in those days. We all knew what Maralinga had been but we didn't know that the British were still actively engaged in testing. That was the reason for being sent there – although we had understood it to be a care and maintenance role.

When I arrived I did not receive any lectures or information about the dangers of radiation or what precautions I should take. In the light of the work I was to do this was an amazing omission. I was not issued with a film badge or any protective clothing. The security areas were colour coded and with my pass I was allowed to visit all of the areas except one. This was a small section of the airfield area. I was endorsed to go there but not to enter certain buildings. No one I knew had that clearance.

As a result of my pervious experiences with Number 5 Airfield Construction Squadron, I was shifted onto working with a crane. In

Avon Hudson (right) at Maralinga

my capacity as a crane operator, I often worked in the forward area
out on the range, beginning at Taranaki. I was assigned to two
boffins, one, a chap called Ken Taylor from the Aldermaston Atomic
Weapons Research Establishment, and the other, Bill Knapp. It was
just starting to get warm when they arrived so it must have been
around about September. I worked with these two scientists building
firing platforms – which had been prefabricated at Salisbury WRE.

These firing platforms were the ones that would cause so much
havoc when it came to spreading radioactive pollution on the range.
We knew nothing of what we were doing at the time. The platform
was a huge steel structure, weighing about 60 tons. It was on four
legs – about as tall as a man – with a lot of gear mounted on top of it.
It had a hole right in the middle where the nuclear device would be
put when it was exploded with conventional explosives. It had a lot
of lead bricks mounted on the top. I worked on it with a crane until
it was completed. The next time I saw the platform was after it
had been blown to pieces. Debris was scattered around but it was
not totally devastated beyond recognition. It had been blown to
pieces with conventional explosives with the nuclear device inside

of it – to test what would happen if the bomb was involved in an accident, like an aircraft taking off and it crashed. Would the bomb explode accidentally? What would happen to the plutonium contained in the nuclear weapon? That's the sort of test that went on there. Of course, at the time we had no idea what it was all for and we were not aware of any danger.

After the Taranaki explosion I had to take the crane there. The whole place was cordoned off and I was escorted in and out. I didn't stay there all that long before I was sent back to Wewak. At Wewak they were testing all of the time. They were testing at other sites called, TM100, TM101, and the Kittens sites.

While I was working at Wewak an incident occurred that I will never forget. Some young British Army chaps came to do a clean-up job at one of the firing sites. They were waiting to go down to the contaminated area when a Health Physics scientist who happened to be on the scene said they were not to go. The dust was so bad. He said: 'They can't go down there until they water the area down and settle the dust because it is too dangerous.' The British Army captain went right off his head and started coming on heavy at this civilian – Health Physics man – who was supposed to be in charge of safety. There was a tremendous argument with a lot of finger waving and carrying on, with arms flying. I heard it all. In the end the captain said to the men: 'Get down there, I am ordering you now, get down there and get the job done.' The poor old Health Physics chap was left floundering, he couldn't do a thing about it, and he was overruled. The men went into the area wearing just their boots, shorts and shirts.

The Health Physics chaps went into these contaminated sites in white protective clothing and rubber boots and white silk gloves, and often they used to have plastic covers over them. They obviously knew more than they were telling us, or the British soldiers. I think it was a cruel and inhumane thing to do. Those young men must have been in the worst sort of danger – the ground there was heavily contaminated and at the time we weren't aware that it was plutonium. As it turned out they were testing these devices with plutonium-239. I have often wondered what happened to those poor young British service men. They were all conscripts, the captain sent them down there knowing how dangerous it was, poor beggars, they must all be dead.

There was another place called 'Rats'. It was not far from the 'Kittens' site. I used to go out there to lift things around, they were blowing things up all the time but I don't know why.

We did a little bit of work one day lifting heavy steel bits after one of the explosions and I don't know when the explosion took place. The Health Physics chaps arrived about 11 am and told us to put a protective suit on before we came into contact with the area around. It was 40 degrees and it was impossible to work with the suits on because the heat was so great. We had to take them off and I was probably better off than most because I was in the cabin of the crane. I wore mine for about half an hour before I took it off and stashed it behind the seat of the crane because it was unbearably hot. I still have that suit today. No one came to check up on us.

The scientists cordoned off an area of about 50 metres in diameter at Wewak. There were no notices for people to keep out but the tape meant that they were required to stay out. I don't know how I came to know this and I can't remember anyone telling me officially. I think that I just found it out by word of mouth while working with other people. That seemed to be the way the camp was run, you learned along the way and it was very much a case of trial and error. I had to go back to Wewak two or three days later and take the crane back to do some more work. A small mobile caravan had been set up. I was told to take the crane down into the area and was told that the Royal Engineers would be there. There were about half a dozen of these along with a bloke with a bulldozer.

Next to where most of the debris lay, a large hole had been dug which was about twelve foot wide and ten foot deep. The majority of the debris had been pushed into the hole and I was sent into the area with the crane to pick up the heaviest pieces, which couldn't be man handled. I often got out of the crane's cabin and walked around the area close to the crane. This was necessary to set up outriggers whenever the crane had to be shifted.

Someone asked about the radioactive contamination and we were told there was very little contamination and it would only be in contact with the tyres of the vehicles. I later found out, by talking with one of the boffins, that the radioactive debris was oxidised in a conventional explosion and scattered all around. The ground around was badly contaminated. We normally didn't touch the tyres of the vehicles but we would have stirred the ground up quite a bit and everywhere we went it was getting dustier as the summer drew on. There were also lots of motor vehicles and digging going on which stirred up a lot of dust – so you can draw your own conclusions.

Over the period of time I got moved here and there and back to the transport depot at the Village. There were some incidents that made me become very suspicious. For example, when one of the British scientists came down dressed in protective suits taking tests while we had no protective clothing whatsoever and one of the young chaps from the British Army remarked that they must know something we didn't know. That sort of thing indicated that there was something amiss. There were a number of other things that occurred and I became more and more suspicious and I was most distrustful of everything and everybody. I learned not to trust anything or anyone any more. I became so suspicious that I started on my own fact-finding mission to try to find out as much as I could, everything I wasn't supposed to know. I began to observe everything I could. As I have an excellent memory it wasn't necessary to incriminate myself by writing a diary.

There was one rule there although I can't say that I know how well it was enforced. We were never allowed to drink water caught off a roof. We were not aware of the reason for this and it was only some time later that we were told of the possibility of radioactivity in the dust. There were a number of water tanks in the village connected to the buildings. These were to gather water for some of the things that needed pure water. I can recall working near one of the tanks and watching a rigger go over and getting water from the tanks. After seeing that, we often used to go and get water from these tanks. It was only later on that we found out by accident that we weren't supposed to use them. One of the fellows in the depot was talking and the subject somehow came up about crook water. We got talking about the rainwater tanks and then we received a blast because we were not supposed to be drinking from them. At that stage, I had only been there a few months and I suppose that is a good indication of how things were only handed around by word of mouth. Often there weren't any written instructions and it was a common occurrence to find out things this way.

Another incident occurred during 1961: there was a Commonwealth census. One morning the Range Commander, Colonel Woolard – the Australian Army Range Commander-in-Charge – arrived at our transport depot early in the morning. There were 28 of us in the transport contingent and we were asked to parade immediately. He told us there was going to be a census and if we were asked any questions in relation to Maralinga we were not to refer to Maralinga at all. He told the married people to make no mention that they were engaged at Maralinga and if there were any questions about who was their employer they were to say that they had been employed by the Colonel. That seemed odd in the extreme and we talked about it among ourselves; they clearly didn't want any publicity or anything recorded about Maralinga. They were more secretive about the Minor Trials than the atomic bomb tests. That is an insight into how Maralinga used to operate. There were many other things that I found out as time went on. I kept my eyes and ears open.

From about August until Christmas 1961, I didn't work continuously in the forward area but I would visit it regularly. It was my job to take tankers of water out there to fill all of the water tanks, which had been set up to service the mobile laboratories. There were five or six mobile laboratories. All of them were air-conditioned and these were serviced by a number of water tanks. We weren't allowed to see inside some of these labs. I believe that 99 per cent of the water delivered to the mobile labs was used for decontamination. The boffins would go into the areas and gather dozens of plastic bags full of samples to test.

I must stress that in all my time at Maralinga, no one gave me any lectures about the dangers of radiation or taught us the differences between the different kinds of radiation. [There are three kinds of ionising radiation, see the chapter 'Radiation: Its nature and the hazards'.] They often lectured us about security, but when it came to taking care of us, for example the dangers of the contaminated forward area – not a bloody word. We only found out on the grapevine after we had been working there for a few months.

Years later I was to learn that the radioactive fallout had fallen right across the site we had to prepare for the minor trials. The whole site was contaminated. It was a radioactive zone, no one told us that. They deceived us. It seems hard to believe they would choose that site, a radioactive one, when they had all the ground area of Maralinga. Why did they have to set up new experiments in a contaminated zone? It was made worse because of the dusty conditions.

In my last six months at Maralinga I began to seriously query what was going on and began to worry about the radioactivity. On one occasion I attended a BBQ with the other chaps. There was generally a friendly rivalry between the British and the Australians and I got talking with some of the British blokes.

One of the British blokes began arguing with me about nuclear weapons. He said to me that we (the Australians) couldn't feed ourselves or defend ourselves and that we were going down the drain, and we were in our death throes. I gave him a blast saying that they (the British) had a few old bombers and bombs and what did they want to do, rule the world with gunboat diplomacy. He then said that they didn't have all their eggs in one basket and that they had something here, and, if they were forced to, they would use it on the bastards. At that point in time, a warrant officer took him aside and told him to be quiet. I was intrigued; I guessed it might have been a nuclear weapon store. It was not long after that I discovered that the building near the airstrip contained operational nuclear weapons, which could have been attached to the Vulcan Bombers stationed at the Edinburgh airbase just outside Adelaide.

I found this out when I later entered the building just before I finished my tour. It was air-conditioned and had a series of air-lock doors to the main hall. I entered the main door and the second door was open so that I could see straight through. The building was about 100 feet long and I could see down at the end of it by the doors that opened onto the airstrip about a dozen nuclear weapons in plastic storage covers. All of these were on trolleys ready to be mobilised. I felt that I had really stumbled on something our government ought to have been aware of.

I strongly believe they were held there without the knowledge of the Australian government. After I left the RAAF I revealed this and I got it recorded in the federal parliament's Hansard. Only a couple of years ago I read, in the press, that the British government had actually lied to many governments around the world about where they had their air bases. They kept their nuclear weapons on these bases without telling the governments. I found all this out in 1961 but it has only just come out in the last couple of years that it was true.

A second thing that concerned me was the waste plutonium which was buried there and which had been brought from Britain. The RAF used to regularly fly Bristol Britannias to Maralinga.

I would generally be in the unloading party for the Britannia aircraft because there was only myself, or Bluey Fisher, who could drive the ten-ton forklift. On this occasion, I was the driver and the plane came in at 3 pm. Usually, there was a security officer, a Commonwealth policeman, and an AWRE representative from Aldermaston on duty. On this occasion, the AWRE boffin was drunk and there was a security officer and a Commonwealth policeman. Of all things on this particular night, it rained which was very unusual. We sheltered under the wing for about ten minutes and then discussed whether we would start. Before we did start, the AWRE bloke put on a turn and complained about having to work under these conditions. He said 'why don't they leave the bloody stuff and dump it in the Atlantic like they used to?' We thought that he was just drunk and that it was the beer talking.

A few days later I was delivering water and got talking to one of the Health Physics people. We were in the office part of the lab. Some of them were willing to talk and I was interested in everything that I could find out. We had taken the stuff to the 'graveyard'. The containers had been about two feet by two feet, weighing around two tons and had been very heavy and we had taken some of them to a position about a half mile from the airfield and some of them were sent to the XA area and some to be dumped [the XA area was a sequence of well-spaced buildings used for assembling the materials for the trials, situated on a five-kilometre stretch of road in the Maralinga Range].

Quite a few similar plane loads came through. One of the containers had Calder Hall written on its sides. We used to get the British newspaper called *News of the World* and I remember this because I had been reading about the Calder Hall nuclear power station. Otherwise it would not have meant anything to me. I understand that Calder Hall was the power station that produced the plutonium that was used to build the British nuclear bombs. Some of their waste was sent out here to be buried, nice one that! Not only did they use our country for bomb tests, they used it for nuclear waste as well. I couldn't believe that the bastards were treating us Australians with such contempt.

Once the stuff was buried, it was never guarded. I found this out years later. I believe this was in direct contravention of the international Memorandum of Understanding, which was in force at the time between the USSR, UK and USA because the plutonium was in a recoverable form and could be obtained by terrorist organisations to make bombs.

We placed the containers in a bulldozed trench about ten feet deep. They were lowered into the hole and a little bit of dirt was placed over it – while I was there the trench was never filled in properly. I believe we simply placed them there and it wasn't for the purpose of permanent burial. During the 1967 clean-up, the trench probably had some concrete placed on top of it. Later, in 1976, I blew the whistle on this shameful fact and after repeated denials by the then Minister for Defence, Jim Killen, the plutonium was eventually recovered and sent back to Britain.

I do believe that there were safety procedures drawn up, but they were never enforced. I once was in a Health Physics caravan and I looked through a book, which seemed to be a safety procedure book, it all seemed to make good sense. I believe there were sufficient safety precautions available at the time but none of these were put into practice. This puts the lie to the suggestion that the British didn't know how dangerous radioactive substances were.

My experiences at Maralinga still make my blood boil. That is why I have spent more than 30 years campaigning – trying to bring it out into the open.

Mike Robinson

I started work as a fitter in the Diesel Repair Shop at the WRE, Salisbury, in 1961. I overhauled diesel generators that were delivered to us from various parts of South Australia. I remember about 20 Coventry Climax generators on their trailers arrived from the Maralinga test sites. I was told to be very careful, as they could be dangerous to my health as they were infested with red-back spiders, ha ha. I didn't know about radiation then.

The Diesel Shop was once the power station for WRE using large diesel generators. There were tunnels underneath the floor for all the pipework. In 1962 these tunnels were filled with various bits of machinery from Maralinga and then concreted over. There are also two dumps of Maralinga waste in the northern end of RAAF Edinburgh.

In July 1961, I was told it was my turn to go to Maralinga for three months to service and repair generators around the area and if I wasn't on the plane on Monday, I would lose my job. I hated it there. Fortunately, I had the use of a Land Rover so that I was able to explore the country. I managed to see where one of the bombs was exploded. There were rows like the spokes of a wheel radiating from a central point. One 'spoke' contained aircraft, I think they were Supermarine Swifts or Attackers. It looked as if the heat from the bomb had travelled in waves, one plane would be okay and the next melted. There were tanks, vehicles and buildings in other rows. I only ever saw one animal around Maralinga, a white dingo who watched me while I worked on an engine out in the Donga.

I heard that a few 'pommy' National Servicemen were planning a trip to Coober Pedy in Land Rovers and I managed to talk my way into being included. We set off in four vehicles travelling to Emu, camping overnight, then through Marbel Creek Station land. We stopped at the homestead to say hello and have a look around. They had a huge mounded building there and we were told that the government had built it in the 1950s. The station personnel were told on certain days they were to stay in it. There were food and water supplies in it. Marbel Creek is a long way from Maralinga or Emu and yet these people were told to shelter. Not so the personnel at the test sites!

We got lost approaching Maralinga on the way back. We eventually came to a sign facing away from us. It said 'Keep Out, Radioactive Area'. I wonder whether any Aboriginal people came that way and what they would have made of the sign.

I left the Diesel Shop in 1963 and moved to the Supersonic Wind Tunnel which was next to RAAF Edinburgh. About 15 years ago, three Canberra bombers were brought to the Aerodynamics Area. One was used as a target for scatter bomb testing then they were sold to private purchasers. Two other fitters and myself spent about a month removing the wings of these aircraft so that they could be transported by road. One went to a Riverland museum, another to a Ballarat museum, and the third to Coober Pedy to be used in a film, I think it was 'Ground Zero' starring Colin Friels who has since had cancer. I have recently been told that at least one of the Canberra bombers was used to fly through the atomic cloud.

'Ground Zero' is a fictional film about a cameraman whose father, also a cameraman, had taken films of the atomic bomb tests at Maralinga. The son goes on to search for the films, which have disappeared, and shows how the authorities went to great lengths trying to cover up everything. At the end of the film there is a long list of some of the people who have died as a result of the tests – my wife's father is one of them.

George Stirna

I came to Australia on 12 December 1958. I got the job of cook in the Officers' Mess at Maralinga and was there for four and a half years.

The kitchen buildings were very high and along the top and bottom were open all the way around. There were sliding windows to try and get a breeze in. They were usually left open as there was no air-conditioning. One afternoon there was a man bulldozing outside. He was there for three days, so the dust was really thick everywhere. I had to wash all the utensils before I could use them each time. I had to keep cleaning the two messes as they were always very dusty.

I was a very healthy person, never smoking and I see no reason why I should now have cancer except perhaps for being at Maralinga. In my view, the fact that I was there later than some has nothing to do with escaping illness as I think the whole place was contaminated.

Edwin Bailey

I served at Maralinga in 1960, during the so-called 'Minor Trials'. The test site at Taranaki, where I spent some time, is still the most heavily contaminated area (even after the 'clean-up').

At the time I worked at the AWRE at Aldermaston in the UK. I was sent to Maralinga as the engineer in charge of weapons assembly. Most of my work was of a secret nature, dealing with weapons of one sort of another. Especially sensitive was my 12 years at Aldermaston, designing and manufacturing nuclear weapons. This period included three and a half months at Maralinga testing them.

The problem of 'How much to say' faced me when I appeared before the Royal Commission in 1984. Before my appearance I had a private meeting with the counsel assisting the Commissioner, which covered what aspects of my work could be revealed. Even so, I was embarrassed by one or two of the questions asked. At one point, discussion took place between the Commissioner, James McClelland and Counsel assisting, if the British government could demand my extradition should I reveal any of their secrets, despite the fact that I had become an Australian citizen. The opinion of the Commission was that they could not – but they were not certain.

Going back to my time at Maralinga. In addition to test firing assemblies similar to the ones on the Essex coast, I would be supervising the assembly of several complete weapons for the 'Vixen B' programme. Test firing the former assemblies could not be done so close to the French coast as they contained radioactive material. One could be sure the French would object! The latter firings were to test the outcome of what is termed 'single point initiation' – several explosive lenses, each of which has to be 'initiated' simultaneously in order that an inwardly directed shock wave collapses the core surrounding the nuclear core of a weapon. The big question was, what if only one explosive lens was initiated? Would there be a nuclear explosion, albeit an inefficient and dirty one? Or would only the high explosive content detonate, scattering the radioactive core as dust or fragments? This test series was to ascertain what would be likely to happen if an aeroplane carrying a nuclear weapon was attacked by enemy fire and one of the lenses was initiated by a bullet or a piece of shrapnel.

Early in 1960 I was invited to be a member of the committee formed to plan the firing programme for the Vixen B set of trials to be held about August of that year. Six firings were held at the Taranaki site, and all six weapons would be suspended from balloons.

After each firing we had to be back at the site to recover equipment. This meant driving through the contaminated area between marker tapes. I was kept busy until early December when I made the explosives assembly area safe and returned to Aldermaston.

When I returned to England I decided to return to Australia as a migrant and brought out my family.

In June 2000 I had a cancerous kidney removed and I am still recovering from the side effects of radiotherapy for cancer of the oesophagus. An MRI. scan has also revealed a small tumour in the adrenal gland and a tiny one in the lumbar region of the spine.

9 – The First Clean-up 1967:
Operation Brumby

A major clean-up of Maralinga, called Operation Brumby, was undertaken by the British in 1967. Major W Cook wrote the Final Report for the AWRE in October 1967. This was classified as 'Confidential' but was unclassified in 1986. In 1967, Sam McGee was a flight lieutenant in the RAF and Officer in Charge in the RAF Maralinga Range Support Unit. He has lived in Australia for some years and has set down his recollections of the 1967 clean-up.

The second account in this chapter comes from Terrence May, who was a truck driver for Shell, delivering fuel and oil to the forward area of the first clean-up of Maralinga. He lived at Maralinga for about a year in 1966, and his story continues that saga of the amazing disregard for the health of the people who, like Sam McGee, worked in these hazardous situations.

Sam McGee

In 1966 I was a Flying Officer in the RAF. I was in charge of the Passenger Section, Air Movements Squadron, RAF Lyneham, England. During a conversation with my boss I mentioned that I would really like a posting to Australia as my wife had many relatives there and I might have a long-lost uncle who had migrated after a gas attack during World War One. Not long after, I was appointed to the rank of Flight Lieutenant. Then I was introduced to Flying Officer Terry Moseley, who had been OC RAF Maralinga Range Support Unit. He was very unwell, having a large growth on his face. I was asked whether I still wanted to go to Australia and if so, I would be in charge of a party of airmen who were to contribute to the clean-up of the mess left by the atomic bomb tests. I was told that the tour of duty would be unaccompanied, that is, without my wife, since Maralinga was in the middle of a vast desert area and no place for women. During this discussion I recall being left with the distinct impression that if I did not agree to let my name [go] forward I need expect no 'preferential treatment' in terms of 'good postings' in the future. It seemed to me that there must have been something against this posting – if what amounted to a form of 'posting blackmail' had to be used. Usually one was not interviewed for a posting, one was just told to go and one went! But on this occasion I was interviewed. The security at the building in London where I had my interview was very tight. It was more stringent than any other I had come across. The upshot was I was posted. I duly arrived in Sydney on 11 November 1966 and was flown to Adelaide and then on to Maralinga on 15 November.

I was delighted to be in Australia, it was a place where everybody wanted to go. Maralinga was, however, a depressing place to work and the RAF men hated it. We had no idea of how long it would take or how big the job was. We were very much aware that we were destined to find out the hard way.

To tell the truth I now feel a little bitter. You see, it is in the past couple of years that I have found out what really happened at Maralinga. This is because when I left the RAF I worked in the Middle East, USA and Mexico for many years. I was out of circulation. However, during the last few years since I have had trouble with my eyes again, the things that happened during my service at Maralinga have been brought to my attention. I started to recall all the things that went on and to understand my involvement in the clean-up.

Starting at the beginning. I regret that I cannot remember anything about the hand-over to me at Maralinga; I was just expected to get on with it immediately. Nothing was mentioned about atomic matters, special precautions, or any particular risks to me or my men. I recall two to three technical people from the AWRE visiting us three to four times during the year of the clean-up. None of them ever mentioned the possibility of residual long-term radiation dangers. However, I am fairly certain the outgoing officer said that he had never been outside the main camp into the forward areas during his year of duty. I spent a little time getting to know people, the most important being the Australian Base Commander Major Alan Gordon.

Wreckage was scattered at various places over the Range. The total area was reputed to be about the size of Ireland. Strangely, no maps were provided to the RAF element of the clean-up group. We had to make up maps from some atlases. We went from site to site looking for wreckage and made arrangements to clear it. It was placed on trucks and carted away for burial, or if pieces appeared to be in good condition it was sent to the Watson railway siding to be railed to WRE Salisbury for eventual sale as scrap. I estimate that we sent about 500 tons of this kind of scrap, none of which was checked for radioactive contamination. Whatever it was we simply picked it up on the Range and took it to Watson where airmen loaded it onto waiting railway wagons.

I know there was other equipment taken back to Adelaide. Things such as: filing cabinets, desks, and beds – they were valuable as they could be sold. My instructions were to rescue anything that was worth salvaging and send it back to Adelaide. It all went to the Department of Supply.

One place that caused me concern was the Emu test site. Here a large area of desert sand had turned to glass or silica from the extreme heat of the blasts. I mentioned this to a visiting technical person and he inspected the area but did not monitor the radioactivity. He reported that he thought it was safe to work there. Eventually the whole area was ploughed up with a bulldozer-cum-scraper so that no trace of glass was left.

We used to drive around for miles and miles looking for wreckage and then we would send the men out and they would bring it back for burial at the main site. Or, if there happened to be a pit nearby it would be more convenient to bury it there. The main burial site was at one of the ground zeros – it was a very large hole looking just like one of the pitted moon craters. Wreckage was brought from all over the range to this one huge hole and buried. At the time no one thought about testing any of the wreckage for radioactive contamination. Nobody was supplied with any type of radiation monitoring device. It never occurred to me to issue any instructions to check materials for contamination.

It is necessary to understand that no written material was made available to me either before my arrival or during my time there. Neither did I have any written orders as to what I was to accomplish, or what was expected of me. In peacetime, air force officers are given 'Terms of Reference'. These are the parameters within which officers are to conduct their operational duties. Nothing like that was provided for me at Maralinga. It quickly became apparent to me and the other officers that we were to use 'common sense' and 'our experience' to get the job done. That year [1967] became a slog – it was a year of unremitting work. I became a sort of commissioned scrap-metal merchant and occasionally I would make a decision about whether to demolish a building or not.

For example, we came across an isolated steel-framed shack clad with very shiny corrugated iron. We discovered the building contained about six-dozen finely machined lead blocks that were obviously designed to act as a shield. Months after we had approached and examined these blocks it occurred to us that in all probability they had been used to shield something contaminated. We felt as if we had walked into real trouble. We also came across a pile of narrow wooden cases. Inside these were 'Bangalore Torpedoes' – pipes three to four feet long, stuffed with dynamite attached to detonators. I had learned that these were notoriously unstable when the dynamite began to 'sweat' with the heat. The cache we found was in a bad way. A day or two later they were carefully removed and the lot blown up. This incident shows the total lack of information we suffered.

On our return to Base I phoned Bill Ferran at Salisbury to report the finding in the shack and ask for disposal instructions. Bill was of the opinion that they were unused reserve blocks and safe to handle. I took this at face value but with a tiny tinge of foreboding and eventually shipped them back to Salisbury for auction sale. I left the building as it was, but I understand that it has now been demolished.

At each site we had to work out what we thought had happened. For example, there was a tower out on the Range. We asked ourselves: 'What the bloody hell would anyone build a great tower in the desert for?' We worked out that something had been suspended. There was a railway line, 500 feet or so long, that went from nowhere to nowhere, that had on it one flatbed truck. We thought it might have been used to sort out a trigger for a bomb.

I was there for 13 months from November 1966 to December 1967. There was no formality about it at all. By November 1967, there was no more stuff to be brought in from the forward area so the bulk of the personnel were sent back to the UK, leaving about 20 or 30 RAF people who were there for the final tidying-up. When Alan Gordon and I were satisfied that everything looked okay and tidy enough, I said: 'Well, there you are, Alan, there's the range back. As far as I am concerned it's Australian again.' I think we shook hands and called the Airlines of SA to send a DC3 to pick us up. The only bit of formality that I insisted on was that I was the last person to get on the last aircraft, so I can say I was the last person out of there.

At the time I was quite pleased with what we had done. When you look at it, it was a bloody great area – the size of Ireland – and we didn't have any proper maps. It was like a circus at times. With the benefit of hindsight I can see it was totally unplanned and ill-thought-out. Now I wasn't led to expect miracles but I did expect a little bit more and I did expect maps!

I have gradually learned that quite a few of the men who were under my command have died and it doesn't make me feel good to think that I might have sent them into badly contaminated areas. I had no instruments with which to check for contamination! I may have given them orders that caused, indirectly anyway, their deaths or sickness. I have to say that doesn't make me feel terrific and it doesn't make me look back with pleasure on what I accomplished or what I achieved. I feel sick about the whole experience and I want to get to the bottom of it and find out what was really going on.

I suppose it's getting a bit late now and I am not looking for revenge – what I am looking for is a bit of help to understand why they did it to us. I think somebody ought to acknowledge or at least say: 'We are sorry.' But from what I gather, people have dismissed the idea – they are not interested.

My knowledge of how an atomic weapon worked was very limited and I kick myself for not asking questions, for not demanding to know about the hazards.

The health problems were not instantaneous. I had problems with my eyes about ten years later. The optical surgeon said I had cataracts because of exposure to radioactive material. I went blind in the left eye about 11 years after leaving Maralinga [and] within 36 hours of noticing I had a problem. I was told that within a year my other eye would go and almost a year to the day I went blind in my right eye. I have had plastic lens implants in both eyes. I now need a cornea replaced in my right eye. Since I have had health problems I have been in contact with others who have had radiation sickness and cataract problems. This experience more or less confirmed a suspicion that had been brewing up in my mind for some time. I decided to find out what I could about the effects of nuclear weapons, and to hear about things that happened to other people. You quickly start to think that the effects will linger on and harm people in the longer term.

I am not surprised that it's been necessary to do the whole clean-up again and a lot more expensively. One hundred million dollars, well I can tell you there was nothing like that spent in what we did! It was all done on the cheap.

I would not be surprised if someone has to go again in a few years and do it again, even after the latest clean-up. From what I have learned, this problem with radioactivity is not going to go away in a hurry. We are stuck with it for years and years. Long after we have all died.

It seems to me that officialdom has been, and continues to be, a case of 'them and us'. They are people who have a vested interest in keeping everything quiet – for the life of me I can't understand why. Some people think it's about money but there's no money that is going to fix my eyes. There's no money that is going to bring back John Shone who was a great friend of mine – he was the nurse there and now he is dead.

There are friends of mine whose children have died. My own daughter suffered from detached retinas as a girl. There was nothing wrong with her eyesight at all, and then suddenly she had detached retinas. There seems to be a nebulous relationship here, a thread of sickness that is passed on from one generation to the next.

I think there are those in government who can do something but they think that our claims will die with us. That's how I feel, they are waiting for us all to die off and in a few more years there won't be any more problems with the atomic bomb 'families'.

Terrence May

I joined the Shell Company and after training in the safe handling of aviation fuels, I went to Maralinga. I was about 21 years old. I transported the fuels needed for the 1996–1997 clean-up of the forward areas – the atomic bomb sites. I used to drive to and from the rail way siding at Watson and distribute the fuels that were needed for the work.

In early November 1966, a British task force arrived to begin the clean-up of the test area.

The dust was very bad and the conditions were hard. During this time I noticed a shower block near the village close to the turn-off to the forward area. I never once saw them being used and I wondered why they were there.

I was only a young man and really didn't know much. I was never told anything about the dangers of exposure to radiation, and I know the task force weren't told anything either. Rumours went around, but generally people didn't speak about any hazards – not to me anyway.

So I went on with my duties oblivious to the fact that I might be at risk because I was working in a dusty and radioactive area. I had a bad experience while I was there. One day I was having a shower getting ready for dinner at the NCO mess when I noticed the drain hole in the shower was blocked so I wiped it with my foot and I found that it was hair blocking it. At this point I grabbed a handful of hair on my head and was horrified to find that it pulled out easily!

The next morning when I awoke I found more hair on my pillow. This alarmed me and I went over to the hospital in the village right away. I was told to wear a hat as the extreme heat was probably causing the problem. It was suggested that I should have my head shaved so that it would strengthen when growing. I did this but still had my doubts. My hair did grow back, but it came back fair and fine. At that stage, of course, I did not know that radiation causes hair loss. I was never tested for contamination, and never given a film badge that recorded how much radiation I had received.

Why were we not told that we were working in a hazardous area? Why weren't we given protective clothing? Why was no information given about the effects of radiation?

Of course, this experience plays on the mind. I have eight lovely grandchildren and I wonder whether my future generations will be affected in any way by my involvement with the clean-up. As far as my health goes, from time to time I have a burning itchy rash that appears on my arms or legs without warning. It lasts from one to three hours before going away. My doctor doesn't know what it is, and naturally you wonder if it could have anything to do with what happened all those years ago.

I am one of the lucky ones – my heart goes out to all those families who have lost loved ones and had their lives destroyed by that horrible place [Maralinga]. I am counting my blessings.'

The Final Report on Operation Brumby gives the official account of what happened during the final clean-up of Maralinga in 1967. There are many matters that cause unease. For example, the way the radioactive material was buried and the conditions under which the men worked. At the Emu site: 'I [Cook] decided to send a party to EMU to carry out final hand scavenging of the areas' (Item 9 of the Report). This was to remove the glazed top-surface of the ground zero sites, caused by the extreme heat of the atomic bomb explosions. After initial felling with explosives, a number of steel towers were dismantled with spanners and cutting torches (Item 23). Cook describes in some detail the precautions the soldiers (Royal Engineers and Royal Pioneer Corps) were said to have taken to guard against radioactive contamination. They were said to have worn protective clothing, they were checked for radioactive contamination and wore film badges to monitor their radioactive exposure (Item 58). But if this had really happened, one would expect that the RAF men would have noticed and they would have asked for the same degree of protection. Sam McGee and Terry May's accounts don't give us much confidence that the men were protected. None of the men appearing in the photographs included in the report were wearing any protective clothing.

This initial clean-up completely failed to restore the desert to what it had been before the tests were conducted. In the next chapter, Alan Parkinson will report on what happened in the latest attempt to restore the site so that it can be safely returned to the Maralinga-Tjarutja people.

10 – The Latest Clean-up

Maralinga, it seems, cannot shake off the legacy of controversy – yet again there is doubt about the future of the region. How safe will it be for the Maralinga-Tjarutja people as they return to their own land? Was even this latest clean-up botched? Was there yet another cover-up? Alan Parkinson, who was part of the engineering group in charge of the clean-up, gives us an account which shows that Maralinga will continue to be a blight on the history of Australia.

Alan Parkinson was first involved in the Maralinga project in 1989. From 1993 to 1998 he was both a member of the Minister's Maralinga Rehabilitation Technical Advisory Committee (MARTAC) and the Commonwealth's representative overseeing the whole project. He was removed from both appointments in 1998, supposedly for questioning the management of the project. He was then an adviser to the Maralinga-Tjarutja people until he withdrew after exposing many shortcomings of the project in 2000.

Alan Parkinson

In early 2000, Senator Minchin [the then Minister for Industry, Science and Resources] discovered Maralinga. At the time he was the minister responsible for the rehabilitation project. In a contrived media appearance, he visited Maralinga and in front of television cameras declared the clean up was complete. In his press release of 1 March 2000, he said: 'Once work is completed in the next month remediating one other minor site and finishing landscaping and revegetating, the Maralinga Rehabilitation Project will have been concluded on time and within its $108 million budget.' Senator Minchin's appearance and media release started yet another chapter in the sorry story that is Maralinga.

A young reporter at the ABC saw the television appearance, reached for her saltcellar and took a large pinch. She had previously interviewed someone who had a long association with the project and noted the evasion when answering questions. She voiced her suspicions to colleagues and the people at ABC Radio National decided that there might be more to the story than appeared in Senator Minchin's platitudes. Gregg Borschmann was given the task of investigating the story.

The Minister himself added further to the controversy with another media release on 13 March 2000. The two-page release was responding to 'unfounded claims on ABC radio that there were safety concerns with the burial of plutonium in deep (ten to 15 m) trenches under a capping of clean soil of at least five metres.' I don't know who suggested that there could be safety concerns – I am not guilty. An interesting feature of the release was the number of times the words 'safe', 'safely' or 'safety' appeared – no fewer than 11 times in less than two pages, and in every case it referred to safety of the work-force, not the long-term safety of the site. Another interesting feature was the word 'deep' when referring to the depth of burial. The code behind which the government has tried to hide considers anything within 30 metres of grade to be near-surface, not deep. Also when the Senator refers to five metres of cover, he fails to add that only two to three metres of that cover is below grade, the rest is a mound above the surface.

Senator Minchin's media releases set the pattern for much of what was to follow. Those two, and many subsequent statements about the project, were distorted, misleading, or simply not true, as shown later in a few of the many examples, and many more can be read in a dissection of statements.

But now I should describe what was planned for the rehabilitation and compare that with what was actually done. I advise that this chapter gives a different story from that peddled by agencies of the Commonwealth government.

In spite of the fact that seven atomic bombs were exploded at Maralinga and two at Emu, none gave rise to the rehabilitation project. It would be wrong however, to assume that the land surface around those ground zeroes is not contaminated. The worst contamination occurs at the Tadje site. This trial has been described as a 'fizzer' and the site was contaminated with cobalt pellets, some of which might remain, and by plutonium, all of which remains. Even though the Australian Radiation Laboratory (ARL) considered Tadje to be 'of concern well into the future' there has been no rehabilitation of that site.

The contamination at Tadje was small-scale compared with what resulted from the hundreds of minor trials. Those trials caused such pollution that the government was eventually forced to act. The sites of greatest concern were Taranaki, which was contaminated with plutonium and uranium, Wewak and the TM sites (TM100 and TM101), which were contaminated with plutonium, and Kuli which was contaminated with uranium. By far the worst contamination was at Taranaki.

The minor trials can be divided into four main types: three were aimed at the development of the bomb (Kittens, Tims and Rats), but the fourth (Vixen) were said to be mainly concerned with the safety of the bomb. Outline descriptions of these trials can be found in Dr John Symonds' book: *A History of British Atomic Tests in Australia*.

The Tims trials were physics experiments to study the behaviour of materials in an assembly under shock from a detonated chemical explosive. There were six trials between mid-October and mid-December 1960, each using about 100 grams of plutonium, none of which was repatriated to Britain. A further series was conducted in September and October 1961, involving about 600 grams of plutonium of which some 500 grams was exhumed from the Airfield Cemetery and returned to Britain in 1979.

The Vixen A trials were detonations and burning of materials, components and assemblies. They were conducted at the Wewak site. The first series, in September 1959, saw two 405-gram rods of plutonium burnt in a petrol fire. About 395 grams were repatriated to Britain in 1959. The second series involved about 570 grams of plutonium in May and June 1961 and none was repatriated.

The Vixen B trials, all of which were conducted at Taranaki, were said to be tests of the safety of nuclear weapons in storage or in transit, but there was an element of weapons development. A nuclear bomb was placed on a large steel structure known as a featherbed, made from heavy steel joists, thick steel plates, and barytes bricks encased in steel, all assembled on a concrete firing pad. The explosive charges were not detonated simultaneously, so there was no nuclear explosion, but the heat of the chemical explosion melted the plutonium and uranium core and shot the molten mix some 800 metres to 1000 metres into the air. The wind then took over and spread the radioactive materials over hundreds of square kilometres in plumes to the northern half of Taranaki.

There were 15 Vixen B trials, but three were calibration rounds at the start of each series, and used only uranium. Of the 12 plutonium trials, three were conducted in September and October 1960. The first used 1300 grams of plutonium, the second and third used 1400 grams each. There were five trials in the second series, conducted in April and May 1961. Each used a little over two kilograms of plutonium. The third series, in March and April 1963, comprised four trials each using about 1900 grams of plutonium. In all of these trials, the plutonium was spread over a wide area and none was repatriated to Britain. In total, the Vixen B trials spread 22.2 kilograms of plutonium, together with 22.4 kilograms of enriched uranium and 25 kilograms of natural or depleted uranium over the Taranaki landscape. Really it is wrong to describe the latter as depleted uranium since it contained a small percentage of U-236, so it would be more correctly described as recycled uranium. That is, it had been through a nuclear reactor.

Information from similar joint British and American trials in the USA in the RollerCoaster series showed that about 20 per cent of the plutonium and uranium went downwards and contaminated the featherbeds and the surrounding soil. The featherbeds were contaminated and so damaged that they could not be used a second time. The British pushed the featherbeds into pits close to the firing pads for disposal. Digging into the hard rock of Taranaki was very difficult, even with the use of explosives, and the pits finished much smaller than was needed. Easier digging was found around the periphery of central Taranaki and two large pits were excavated at both the eastern and western ends, and three at the northern edge of central Taranaki.

In 1967, the British Army conducted a final clean-up of the Maralinga range under the code name Operation Brumby. Major W Cook reported on the clean-up. According to that report: 'The operation was progressing well at the beginning of July, and every effort was made to complete the major tasks for inspection by the AWTSC, and assuming that they would be satisfied, to complete all the remaining tasks and withdraw from the Range, and Australia, by the end of the month.' The AWTSC was a committee established by the Australian government to advise on the safety of the atomic trials in Australia. This paragraph suggests that Australia had no representation on site during Operation Brumby.

The main activities of Operation Brumby were ploughing and mixing soil at Taranaki, the TM sites and Wewak in an attempt to reduce the radioactivity (by dilution) to what was considered an acceptable level. Some parts of central Taranaki were still very highly contaminated and 4200 m^2 of soil were spread over the offending areas.

Radioactive debris was disposed of in 32 pits around the site, 21 of which were at Taranaki. It was reported that 19 of them were covered with 300-millimetre-reinforced concrete caps extending a metre beyond the pit boundary on all sides. The other two pits simply had a plug of concrete placed over them to finish at ground level (which was a rock surface). High cyclone mesh fences were erected around the pits containing the contaminated debris at Taranaki and the TM sites, and at the Airfield Cemetery. Other debris, which was supposedly not contaminated, was disposed of in some 60 other pits, and in the crater left by the Marcoo bomb, which was filled and covered.

Committee members arrived on site on 8 July 1967 and left on 10 July 1967, and in that period they inspected the Maralinga range and visited Emu. According to Cook: 'The committee was extremely satisfied with the operation and on Sunday [9 July], the Chairman, Professor Titterton, spoke to the Force and thanked them for the work they had done. A statement saying that they were satisfied was given by the Committee to the British government, and a formal handover document is now in course of preparation.'

The committee advised the Australian government that the site was in an acceptable condition for it to be abandoned by Britain. The two governments signed an agreement in September 1968, by which Britain was released from all further responsibilities for the site.

Another British report by Pearce gives some information on the residual radioactive contamination of Maralinga and Emu (Pearce 1984). Although some in Commonwealth government ranks have claimed that the Pearce Report was used to guide the clean-up, that is not so. Even a cursory glance at the amount of plutonium said to be buried in the Taranaki pits would show that the information was very suspect. The report said that 20 kilograms of plutonium was buried in those 21 pits. This would have meant there was only two kilograms spread over the hundreds of square kilometres to the north of that site. Other errors were found as the project progressed.

In the mid-1980s, scientists from the ARL visited the site and monitored the surface radioactivity. They found that the site was not in an acceptable state and arranged for additional fencing to be erected, particularly around the northern part of Taranaki and around the TM sites.

In 1984, the Australian Commonwealth government established a Royal Commission to inquire into the status of both Emu and Maralinga. The President of the Commission was Mr Justice McClelland, a former Labor government minister. The inquiry found that previous clean-ups were inadequate, and in some ways made future attempts at clean-up more difficult. A key recommendation was that Britain should pay for the site to be cleaned up sufficiently to allow unrestricted access by the Aboriginal population.

The Australian government then set up a Technical Assessment Group (TAG) to investigate many aspects of the site and the lifestyle of Aborigines, and to develop options for the clean-up. An aerial survey of the contaminated areas was conducted jointly by Australia and Britain in 1987, and this was backed up by a ground survey by technicians from the ARL. The TAG reported to the Australian parliament in 1990 by tabling a report, which contained some 30 options for rehabilitation of the site.

There followed a period in which the government reviewed the options and negotiated with stakeholders and with Britain. While the main consideration would have been to make the site safer, the estimated cost must have been a prime factor in discussions. In the event, a halfway scheme was adopted between simply fencing the contaminated area and scraping up all of the contaminated soil for burial. So the latest clean-up was to be a compromise from the outset, driven by cost.

By 1993, agreement had been reached between the Commonwealth government, the South Australian government and the traditional owners, the Maralinga-Tjarutja. They agreed that the clean-up would comprise: removal of plutonium-contaminated soil from areas that had been ploughed during Operation Brumby (2.1 km^2) for burial in trenches at the three contaminated sites; importation of clean soil to cover the scraped areas and revegetation of those areas; treatment of the 32 pits containing contaminated debris by in situ vitrification (ISV); sorting through the 60 or so other pits which were reported to contain non-radioactive debris, removal of any contamination that might be found and disposal of it to the main burial trench; and erection of a fence around the contaminated area to the north of Taranaki to prevent access.

Later, the notion of fencing gave way to a line of posts placed at 50-metre intervals. The posts, referred to as boundary markers, carry signs, which advise the Aboriginals that the enclosed land is safe for hunting and transit, but they should not make permanent camp there.

Other options were considered for the disposal of the radioactive debris. One was to exhume the pits before removing soil and place the debris in a concrete lined sub-trench at the bottom of the main burial trench. Another was to exhume the pits and place the debris in a borehole 100 metres to 200 metres deep. Yet another option was to pump either cement or chemical grout into the pits to immobilise the contents, but this option was never given much credence. Consideration was also given to further mixing of the topsoil to dilute the radioactivity and yet another was a novel technique by which plutonium could be separated from the soil.

Following approaches by the Australian government, Britain made an ex gratia payment of £20 million (about $44 million) towards the estimated $104 million cost. A paltry sum when compared with the cost of the trials, which contaminated the site, and far from McClelland's recommendations.

The TAG considered the potential dose to an Aboriginal living a semi-traditional lifestyle on the range and proposed the risk of one in 10,000 of contracting a cancer by age 50 as a criterion to guide the clean-up. This led to an estimated dose of five milliSieverts per annum, which can be compared with the annual dose of one milliSieverts per annum allowed for a member of the public. The dose of five milliSieverts per annum could be encountered by an Aboriginal living a semi-traditional lifestyle in areas contaminated at three kilo-Becquerels of americium-241 per square metre, equating to about 25 kBq of plutonium/m^2. The proposition was accepted by the Maralinga-Tjarutja.

The Commonwealth Department of Primary Industries and Energy (DPIE) was made responsible for the clean-up, but there was no regulatory organisation in being at that time. In 1993, the DPIE set up MARTAC to advise the Minister on the project. Most of the six members of the committee had backgrounds in nuclear science, nuclear engineering or radiation protection. They met three or four times a year and, while their prime responsibility was advisory, they actually defined the project.

MARTAC reconsidered the clean-up criteria and estimated the level of radioactivity, which could lead to a dose of five milliSieverts per annum. They agreed with the basic three kiloBecquerels Am-241/m^2 criterion for the clean-up. The task was then to establish a level of contamination for the soil removal boundary. At a meeting of just one half of MARTAC, the level of contamination for the soil removal boundary at Taranaki was set at 40 kBq Am-241/m^2 but additional criteria were needed to deal with millions of contaminated particles and fragments. In practice, parts of the soil removal boundary were marked at lower than the 40 kBq contour. Strangely, this does not seem to have been done between the north-west and north plumes because some fragments, such as a lead brick contaminated with about 200 kBq Am-241, remained just beyond the boundary. As explained later, the suppression of dust during soil removal at Taranaki was quite inadequate and when an Health Physics technician went to remove the lead brick after soil removal was complete, he found it was covered by about 600 millimetres of soil.

Application of the clean-up criterion to the whole area contaminated above three kiloBecquerels Am-241/m^2 would have required the removal of 120 km^2 of soil at Taranaki, so a compromise was agreed. This was to remove only the most contaminated soil for burial. Since the contaminated areas at the TM and Wewak sites were very much smaller than at Taranaki, and there would be no boundary markers, all of the contaminated soil above the end-state criterion would be removed and buried.

A contract was let to ARL in 1994, to delineate the soil removal boundary at the three plutonium-contaminated sites and also to specify the Health Physics policy for the project. ARL also accepted appointment as the regulator for the Health Physics aspects of the project, but strangely not for the site remediation work. In fact they never formally endorsed the clean-up criteria, always referring to them as MARTAC criteria. Even after ARL was absorbed into the Australian Radiation Protection and Nuclear Safety Agency (ARPANSA) in February 1999, the criteria were still known as MARTAC criteria.

The Department [DPIE] invited companies to register interest in providing engineering and project management and Health Physics services to the project. From 38 registrants, three companies were selected and invited to submit formal tenders. The tenderers were given as much detail as possible about the project requirements, and this was supplemented by a two-day visit to the site. After due consideration of the tenders and discussions with each tenderer, a contract was awarded to Australian Construction Services (ACS), which was part of the Department of Administrative Services.

The first work was to erect a construction camp for the site workforce and upgrade the site infrastructure – providing electricity, water supply and sewerage, and to upgrade the roads to the work sites. The Watson siding was also upgraded, but no sooner had the site buildings and heavy equipment been off-loaded, than the railway management closed the siding.

The next work was to excavate trenches 15 metres deep at the three main sites, and then to collect the contaminated soil at those sites for burial in the trenches. The soil removal phase of the project started in 1996 and was completed in early 1998. By far the largest trench was at Taranaki – 205 metres by 140 metres in area at the lip, and 15 metres deep. This gave an effective capacity for burial of 285,000 m^2 of contaminated soil with an allowance for a cover of three metres of clean soil to grade and a further two to three metres above grade.

Soil collection was basically a large earth moving exercise with an overlay of health physics. The plant and other vehicles to enter the contaminated areas were modified to protect the operators from radiation. The cabs were sealed and ventilated with filtered air.

The Taranaki site was marked out in 40 lots. Scrapers collected the soil from the 1.6 km^2 within the soil removal boundary and transported it to the burial trench. After the scrapers had removed the first layer of soil, the AHPT surveyed the ground surface to check whether or not the new surface met the clean-up criterion. If not, the scrapers would make a second, third, or even a fourth cut. Some parts of central Taranaki failed to meet the criterion even when the scrapers and graders had reached bedrock. A road sweeper removed the final remnants of contamination, and even then some pockets had to be loosened by a worker wielding a pick so that the soil and small rocks could be sucked into the sweeper.

When the AHPT considered the clean-up criterion had been met, ARL technicians conducted a confirmatory survey. If ARL was satisfied that the clean-up criterion had been met a clearance certificate was granted for that lot. In nearly all cases the lot met the criterion, but in some a concession was granted by ARL. An estimated 2.6 kilograms of plutonium was removed from Taranaki in the soil removal exercise.

In general, all lots satisfied the clean-up criterion, but the soil removal exercise at Taranaki should not be described a success. It was a constant complaint that dust suppression was quite inadequate. Although the contractor spent a great deal of effort watering the lots before the scrapers took the first cut, that effort was really wasted. A photograph published in the *Advertiser* and the *Daily Telegraph* on August 2002 showed how dry the soil really was when it was deposited in the burial trench. But that was not the worst of the dust raising. No matter how much watering was done before the scrapers moved in, it was never enough. After the first cut was taken, the remaining surface was dry. The hot winds then made their presence felt and tens, perhaps hundreds of thousands of tonnes of contaminated soil simply blew away beyond the soil removal boundary. Since that soil was usually less contaminated than the soil just beyond the boundary it covered more contaminated soil. In some ways that was an advantage, but any estimates of dose, which could be received on the north side of Taranaki, should take account of that underlying radioactivity. In fairness to the contractor, before soil removal transferred to the other two sites, a 'lessons learned' meeting was held. The outcome of that meeting resulted in a change in work procedure and while watering continued before the scrapers did their work, the scraped area was also watered after soil removal. This was a far more satisfactory method and there was no dust carry-over at TM and Wewak.

The boundary markers around Taranaki were generally placed at the three kiloBecquerels Am-241/m^2 contour but for operational reasons and to prevent any future confusion, the markers were placed along existing tracks, which were sometimes barely discernable. As a consequence, although some 120 km^2 remains contaminated above the end-state criterion, the area enclosed by the boundary markers is closer to 450 km^2 and this includes the seven sites where nuclear bombs were exploded.

The Commonwealth also let a contract to Geosafe Corporation of the USA to develop the ISV process to match the Taranaki geology. The purpose of ISV is to use electricity to convert the pit contents into a stable glass-like rock, which immobilises the plutonium for hundreds of thousands of years. Some two metres of clean overburden

[soil] was placed over the pit and up to 4.5 Mw of electricity was used to melt this overburden and the underlying contaminated material in the pit. The electricity was delivered through four graphite electrodes supported by the steel hood. The electrical energy was converted to heat energy to melt the overburden. The heat then advanced down into the pit to melt the pit contents. The electrodes followed the downward progress of the molten pool until all of the pit contents were treated.

The ISV technology has to be adjusted to match the geology of the place of application. The development for Maralinga started with very small samples melted in a crucible in the USA. It graduated to small-scale trials conducted in the Maralinga Village, and culminated in two engineering-scale trials conducted at Taranaki. The first of the engineering-scale trials contained two kilograms of uranium swarf, and the second contained two kilograms of uranium swarf plus a steel plate, which was contaminated with about three grams of plutonium. Each of these melts weighed a little over four tonnes, which can be compared with a full-scale melt of 400–500 tonnes.

Even though the final trial contained some unmelted steel at the base, MARTAC and the Department personnel all agreed that ISV would be suitable for the treatment of the Taranaki pits. The Commonwealth let a contract in mid-1996 to Geosafe Australia to design and build the ISV plant, and then to use it to treat the Taranaki pits. In selecting ISV, the Department said, 'The ISV technology was selected over exhumation and reburial at the Taranaki site because of advantages of improved occupational, public and environmental safety, and superior containment of radioactive materials in the glassy product.'

As work proceeded, further study resulted in modifications to the original scope of work. For cost reasons, ISV was restricted to the 21 pits at Taranaki. The pits at Wewak and the TM site, including the Tietkens Plain Cemetery, were exhumed and the debris placed at the bottom of the burial trenches at those sites. Some pits in the Airfield Cemetery were also exhumed and the radioactive debris was transported to Taranaki for burial. Lumps of uranium on the surface at Kuli were collected and buried and the central area of Kuli was scraped and the soil buried.

In mid-1997, ACS was sold to a private firm, Gutteridge Haskins and Davey (GHD). This was acceptable because their part of the project was coming to an end except for the provision of Health Physics services and camp management. But the purchase meant that a company that had not made the final six considered to manage the project became project manager.

In the meantime, soil removal was well in progress, but as soil was scraped from central Taranaki a great deal of steel and other debris was uncovered. It became apparent that the pits were very much larger than had been understood from the British reports. For example, Pit 10 at the western end was about five times larger than the British reported. Pits 5, 8 and 11 on the northern edge of central Taranaki turned out to be one very large pit. Later it was found that the caps of two pits were some metres from the pits they were supposed to cover. This discovery showed how difficult it is to detect plutonium. ARL had granted clearance certificates for those two lots but there was a huge amount of plutonium-contaminated debris only a few centimetres below the surface. The real impact of the larger-than-expected size of the pits was that ISV would cost more to complete than had been quoted. So Geosafe was asked to provide a revised estimate of cost.

By the end of 1997, the ISV equipment had been built and tested, and was ready to be shipped to the site when the Department did a very strange thing. Some would say a very stupid thing. On the day after asking Geosafe for the revised estimate, the Department told them that GHD would be taking over the management of that phase of the project.

This take-over had been discussed in three meetings held in secret between the Department and GHD without Geosafe's knowledge. Indeed, the Commonwealth's Representative, overseeing the whole project, was not informed about the meetings and was deliberately excluded. In fact, according to the Department, he was so opposed to the appointment of GHD to manage the ISV phase that he was simply removed from the project and from MARTAC. Nobody from the Department was interested in why he was opposed to the appointment. This extraordinary event signalled problems for the project, but nobody in the Department cared. The person who was mainly responsible for these changes said he was about to leave the project so it was somebody else's problem.

The conduct of the most expensive and complex part of the whole project was decided by two people from the Department and two from GHD. The Department personnel had little knowledge of the project and had only witnessed a half-hour inspection of some of the ISV equipment. Nobody from GHD had even seen the full-scale equipment, and none of the four had been involved in any way in the three-year development programme mentioned above. In short, GHD were not qualified for the work and the Department did not bother to check their credentials. Whatever happened in those meetings remains both a mystery and a secret because apparently there are no records. Although Senator Lyn Allison (Democrat, Victoria) asked for records of the meetings, what she received was a list of topics to be discussed at one meeting. The list had only one item relevant to the discussion of the GHD take-over and that said: 'Ask GHD to outline reasons why they consider their management of the ISV phase of the Maralinga Rehabilitation Project advantageous to DPIE.' We shall never know what they said. All very strange.

Even more strange was the fact that GHD was appointed Project Authority as well as Project Manager. While appointment as Project Manager should have required them to have some understanding and experience in the field, appointment as Project Authority required them to have a detailed knowledge of the technology. The situation was made even worse because the Department had no one in their ranks with any understanding at all of what was required. So Geosafe, the world's experts in ISV, found themselves reporting to a company which had absolutely no knowledge of the process or the equipment while being contracted to a client (the Department) which also had no expertise. From that point on, partly because of ignorance of the technology and partly because of the way that the take-over was handled, the project had a very uncertain future. The Department claimed that they reviewed the management of the project and decided that they would be more comfortable if it was managed by a large company. In other words, the system that had been in place for the past four years was changed. Their claim is further spurious because the management of the ISV phase was more in the form of a joint venture between Geosafe and their major contractor, Amec – the third-largest engineering company in the world (far larger than GHD) and one with an international reputation for sound project management.

At the same time as all this clandestine business was in progress, the government was seeking ways to minimise the cost of this part of the project. This was towards the end of 1997, seven months before ISV operation started on site. The Department considered various schemes to exhume some of the pits, sort the contents, bury some of the debris and treat the remainder with ISV. This was known as the hybrid option and was announced to the South Australian government and the Tjarutja in September 1998 – an announcement that was not endorsed by the Tjarutja. Amazingly, the sorting was done on the basis of size, not level of radioactivity. The larger pieces were to be treated by vitrification and the smaller items and soil buried, even though the latter could be more radioactive. The government then started exhuming eight large pits around the periphery of central Taranaki, while 13 inner pits were being vitrified.

Another surprising fact was that a basic requirement of any contract was omitted from the contract with Geosafe. The contract did not contain any statement as to what Geosafe had to meet and there were no criteria by which the outcome of ISV could be gauged. Although MARTAC had proposed some criteria, amazingly they were not included in the contract. Even so, every melt satisfied both the contract and the non-contractual criteria. Ten melts had been completed before there were any criteria agreed with Geosafe and all of the following melts also satisfied those criteria and the contract.

As treatment of the pits continued, the lack of knowledge of ISV on the part of the Department and GHD became all too apparent. Into this void stepped MARTAC, which had expectations that were not contractual and were constantly changing. Even though all members of the committee had supported the recommendation to adopt the ISV process, agreeing it was the best solution available, some started to express concerns about its effectiveness. Instead of asking the

Project Manager to confirm the effectiveness of ISV, the advisory committee took it upon itself to act as quality manager for the project. But instead of using a drill to take core samples of the blocks for laboratory analysis, they started to break up the blocks searching for evidence or otherwise of compliance with the non-contractual criteria. They found it was not an easy task to break up the blocks even with a hammer fitted to the arm of a large and powerful excavator. One factor in particular that received a lot of attention was unmelted steel in the block, in spite of the fact that there was never a requirement to melt the steel. Instead the criterion said: 'There should be a high degree of confidence that the contaminated soils and debris within the pits are completely melted or encased in the vitrified product.' Particular criticism was levelled at the unmelted steel found in the block of Pit 15, but the project record shows that GHD instructed Geosafe to stop melting that pit.

On 21 March 1999, as treatment of Pit 17 was almost complete, there was an explosion within the pit and molten glass was spewed some 50 metres from the pit, causing extensive damage to the hood in the process.

Geosafe conducted an investigation into the possible cause of the explosion, and GHD arranged for an audit of the Geosafe report. On 23 June 1999, the Department announced that it was abandoning any form of vitrification, claiming that there was no conclusive evidence as to the cause of the explosion and stating that it was unsafe to continue. This decision was made several months before the two reports were delivered in October and December 1999. Although the reports did not agree as to the most likely cause of the explosion, they did agree that it was caused by something in the pit and not by the ISV process. The Geosafe report concluded that an explosive in the pit caused the incident. The audit report concluded that a more likely cause was a drum of volatile material.

Having abandoned vitrification, the Department was left with the exhume-and-bury option for all pits. But instead of segregating the debris they simply dropped it into a bare hole in the ground. Quite unnecessarily, they then broke up all of the ISV blocks and placed the pieces over the debris as a kind of barrier. This was covered by a layer of soil and some plastic sheeting, which the Department claimed has a life of a few thousand years! The hole was then covered with about five metres of soil, which extends two to three metres above the surface – so the top of the debris is actually within three metres of the surface. The Tjarutja dissociated themselves from the decision simply to exhume and bury the debris.

Among the many spurious claims by the Department, was one that the decision to exhume and bury the debris was made partly because the amount of plutonium in the pits was less than had been expected when ISV was proposed. But they had already started work on the hybrid scheme several months before they had any indication of the plutonium content of the pits. An early estimate of the amount of plutonium in the Taranaki pits was 2.2 kilograms according to a British report received in Australia in 1987. That estimate was in turn based on earlier reports that quoted one to three kilograms. Those early estimates, supported by the RollerCoaster data, were accepted seven months before the contract was signed with Geosafe, as shown in the minutes of the MARTAC meeting in November 1995, which concluded that there would be between 2.2 and 4.4 kilograms. The Department later acknowledged the amount of plutonium to be two kilograms, so validating the initial estimates. Later the Department claimed the amount was less than one kilogram, but nine concrete pads that had been buried in Pits 5 and 11 and were contaminated with possibly one and a half kilograms of plutonium seem to have disappeared and do not appear in the record of burials.

Since every member of MARTAC and all other parties agreed that ISV was a far superior waste form, one could have expected that when that process was cancelled the Department would take the next-best option. This would have been to segregate the debris so that it would be readily retrievable should a future administration not accept the simple burial option. They could not revert to one of the original proposals (to place the debris in a concrete-lined sub-trench at the bottom of the main trench), but they could have placed it in a concrete vault so that it was segregated and retrievable. Also, the debris could have been disposed of in a deep borehole. But they were looking for the cheapest option, and chose to bury the debris in a shallow grave at the site.

With that knowledge, Senator Minchin went to the site and declared it to be safe and the project complete. And it was then that ABC Radio National took a keen interest.

After speaking to 20 people or more, Gregg Borschmann heard about me and we got together. We exchanged numerous telephone calls, faxes and e-mails, and Gregg spent three days at my home in Canberra, looking through papers in my possession. He then switched on the tape recorder and fired many questions in my direction. He also contacted many others who had knowledge of Maralinga or radiation matters. Some would not be interviewed. The outcome was a 50-minute programme in the Background Briefing series, which exposed some of the shortcomings of the project. It also reported the strange events that led to GHD being appointed to manage something for which they were totally unqualified.

That programme sent the Commonwealth agencies into orbit. The first statement was released the following day. In an astonishing claim, the Chief of ARPANSA said: 'Claims that the clean-up of Maralinga is not to world's best practice are not well founded.' A cheap solution that would not be tolerated in any other Western country is world's best practice? A couple of years later, an even more astonishing claim was made by Science Minister Peter McGauran who said in a radio interview that what was done at Maralinga exceeded world's best practice!

Senator Allison took a great interest in the project and posed many questions in Senate hearings in May 2000. Those hearings exposed the inadequacies of some of the public servants responsible for the clean-up – their shortcomings in technical and radiation matters were exposed for the world to see. Many of the answers to questions were simply not true. Many questions were ducked, and many answers were distorted to hide the truth. It was during the second day of the hearings that Senator Minchin claimed that cost had nothing to do with the cancellation. He said: 'Can I refute the scurrilous suggestion which I see floating around in the media that this decision was made on cost grounds.' But this is totally at odds with project papers leading up to the decision. For example, one paper stated quite clearly: 'The recent consideration of alternative treatments for ISV for these outer pits has arisen as a result of the revised estimate for ISV being considerably above the project budget.' This in spite of the fact that there were ample funds still available in the project budget for even the most expensive ISV option.

The government constantly says that the burial option is consistent with the Code of Practice for the Near-surface Disposal of Radioactive Waste in Australia (1992). Sometimes they say that what has been done satisfies the code and sometimes they say they did not need to satisfy it. Three of the five authors of the code said that it was not applicable to the Maralinga clean-up; the other two were public servants and would not comment. Whether or not they were required to satisfy the code is immaterial because it is a fact that not a single requirement has been met. It cannot even be said to have been used as a guide. For example, there was no environmental impact statement, no water management plan, and no radiation management plan. Most importantly, since the Commonwealth hopes to off-load the site to the Maralinga-Tjarutja, the code states: 'The [disposal] site should not be located in an area where land owner-ship rights or control could compromise retention of long term control over the facility.'

Sometimes, the Department and ARPANSA describe the work at Maralinga as an intervention and say that this requires them only to improve the situation. While accepting that explanation, should they not have improved the situation as much as possible within the constraints of the budget? Should they not have spent the money so that the improvements were the best that could be achieved? If the intention was simply to improve the situation, then there are far cheaper ways to achieve that end and obtain a better result, and they did not need to spend $40 million on an aborted scheme to do so. Better still, they could have retained the best technology available – ISV, and applied it without the interference that was apparent. But in saying that, it would have been wiser in retrospect to have exhumed the pits and then vitrified the debris.

In July 2001, the government published a discussion paper seeking public comment on the process to find a site suitable for a store for intermediate-level waste in readiness for eventual disposal in a deep geological repository. Twice that paper states that long-lived radio-active waste, whether low-level or intermediate-level, is not suitable for near-surface disposal. But that is exactly what has been done at Maralinga. Further, when the Commonwealth announced that it was seeking a company to find a site suitable for the establishment of a store for intermediate-level waste, they noted that the waste would include americium and uranium – these are two of the contaminants at Maralinga, plus of course the far more hazardous plutonium. The Commonwealth proposes to store these wastes until a deep geological repository is available. And yet the Commonwealth agencies continue to claim that the world's best practice is to shallow-bury debris contaminated with americium, uranium and plutonium in a bare hole in the ground in totally unsuitable geology at Maralinga. There is no consistency in the government's approach to the disposal of radioactive waste and the double standards are quite evident. What hope is there for the future?

11 – France: We are not alone

Bruno Barrillot

translated by Jennifer M T Carter

Veterans and victims of the
French nuclear tests speak out

**Observatoire des armes nucléaires françaises,
Lyon, France.**

Between 1960 and 1996, nearly 70,000 people took part in at least 210 nuclear tests carried out by France, first in the Sahara then at Moruroa and Fangataufa atolls from 2 July 1966. The great majority of these men weren't volunteers: they had been sent to the test sites to carry out their national service. They were no more informed of the risks than were the Algerian and Polynesian workers employed for subordinate tasks.

We were young, carefree and happy to take part in this great adventure of the bomb. And besides, we were off to the other side of the world at the State's expense! And anyway, what could have been more reassuring when the written instructions given by the army to its men falsely stated that after the bomb exploded, there would be nothing to fear from radiation! (Barrillot 2003, p. 5)

Neglect and accidents in the Sahara

Today, however, veterans are wracking their memories for things that have been forgotten for many years. At Reggane (in the Sahara), where France detonated its first bomb into the atmosphere on 13 February 1960, military authorities generously had 'one pair of glasses per 40 men' distributed among the soldiers.

Two years later, a few weeks after the end of the Algerian War, France inaugurated a new firing technique, underground, in the side of a mountain – the Tan Afela in the south Sahara. This was intended as a great spectacle and took place in the small hours of 1 May 1963. In order to give the event a higher profile, the army invited two of General de Gaulle's ministers – Messieurs Pierre Messmer and Gaston Palewski – to be present. Surrounded by almost 2000 men, they were to witness the tremendous spectacle of a mountain shaken by the brutal impact of the explosion.

Unfortunately, an unforeseen catastrophe occurred: onlookers watched in disbelief as Tan Afela split open. An enormous black cloud escaped from its side and began to blot out the sky above the crowd of spectators. Panic reigned. Those who were there will remember a debacle that brought no credit at all on the army. Officers were the first to run away while simple soldiers were 'forgotten' for hours in the radioactive storm. As for the PLBT (Working Classes of Lower Taouat) – the Tuareg auxiliaries employed by the French to do the menial work – they were abandoned to their fate.

The choice of French Polynesia

In 1962, however, Algeria gained its independence. The Franco-Algerian independence treaties had agreed that the French army could continue its Sahara tests for five years, to give it time to find an alternative solution. For several years it had withdrawn to other climes, to French Polynesia.

What is more, the military had realised that the underground tests in the Sahara were by no means conclusive. They therefore decided to revert to atmospheric testing despite France being a signatory to the 1963 ban on tests being conducted in the atmosphere. We had to wait until 1974 for France to put an end to atmospheric tests – after an unprecedented campaign carried out through diplomatic channels and public opinion.

It would be tedious to list the accidents and unforeseen incidents that occurred and reoccurred during this period, provoking radioactive fallout, not only on military personnel but also on the islands and atolls neighbouring Moruroa and Fangataufa. It is enough to say that with 45 blasts into the atmosphere, Polynesia and neighbouring archipelagos experienced the equivalent of 675 Hiroshimas.

The associations are formed

In 1995, when everyone hoped to have seen the last of the bomb, the renewal of testing, undertaken without any consultation by [French president] Jacques Chirac, unleashed fury among the Polynesians. Because their opinion had never once been asked over a period of 30 years, the ONG [the traditional people of Tahiti], backed by the Evangelical Church – the dominant religious persuasion in the archipelagos – embarked upon a process of discussion during a sociological investigation being carried out by two Dutch experts among ex-Moruroa workers.

'Moruroa e tatou' [Moruroa and us] was the name chosen by the association of former workers that was created in Tahiti on 4 July 2001, a date close to the 35th anniversary of the first French bomb over Moruroa Atoll. A year later, the association had 1200 members, constituting a record.

At the same time in France, while a debate on 'Gulf Syndrome' raged in the media, nuclear test veterans – professional soldiers, civilian members of the Atomic Energy Commission, civilians employed by subcontractors, and National Servicemen who had served in the Sahara or Polynesia – formed an association on 9 June 2001. Today this association has nearly 1000 members.

The explanations for this awakening of witnesses, almost 40 years after the event, are complex and manifold. Many felt bound by the secrecy imposed upon them, but the main reason is probably simpler: most of these people were very young men. They were caught up in the great bomb adventure. The immediate risks were not obvious and their consequences were only revealed many years later. But for all that, the majority of veterans and former workers maintain, no one had told them a thing.

Serious health problems

It was illness that inspired the veterans to form an association. According to a medical enquiry conducted among members of the veterans' association, 93 per cent of them claim to be in poor health. 'Nearly 30 per cent of declared illnesses are cancerous', states Dr Jean-Louis Valatx, president of the association, a doctor and director of the National Institute for Health and Medical Research [French title: Institut nationale, de la Santé et de la recherche médicale], 'whilst the national average for a similar age sample of the French population approaches 17 per cent.' But many other non-cancerous ailments afflict the veterans: skin and bone diseases, and diseases of the cardiovascular system. Many veterans have also had difficulty in having children. Some of them were even recommended by military doctors to wait a few years before having children. Not all of them followed this advice and many deplore the death of their first child and the malformation of the others.

Several veterans – or their widows – have tried to get the military authorities to research these illnesses or deaths. All they have received from the military health services are contemptuous replies, unworthy of doctors bound by their Hippocratic oath.

Today, faced with this contempt and with information being withheld under the pretext of the sacrosanctity of military secrets, anger is making itself heard. 'Let them keep all the secrets about the bomb – they don't interest us in the slightest,' the veterans exclaim. 'But when our health is at risk, when the future of our children causes us daily anguish, it is impossible not to take serious action.'

Justified requests for compensation and claims for pensions take second place to the thirst for information, the desperate need to learn the truth. The associations are urging their government to open up the nuclear test archives 'because we have the right to know'.

In January 2002, a conference was organised at the Senate in Paris. The associations had invited representatives from their English, American, Australian, New Zealand and Fijian colleagues and these all came to France to present the initiatives taken on their behalf by their own governments. It was a way of showing how far behind the times France is, and to what degree it is a prisoner of the dogma we have heard repeated over 40 years: that French nuclear testing was absolutely harmless.

For further information: www.obsarm.org.

12 – One Man's Burden

Campaigning for justice

Avon Hudson became suspicious of the rotten core of the bomb business while he was at Maralinga working on the Minor Trials in 1960–1961. Working largely alone, he has done more than anyone else over a period of more than 30 years to uncover the truth about the many cover-ups, lies and the deceitful ways in which the Australian and British armed forces and civilians were treated by the Australian and British governments. He gave evidence to the Royal Commission into the British Nuclear Tests in Australia because he was concerned about the negligence that occurred, and the continuing danger to human life.

This is the personal history of one man's determination to uncover the truth.

Avon Hudson Nuclear Veterans' Advocate

From the day I left Maralinga in 1961, I began to reflect on my work there. As the years went by I became increasingly concerned about the plutonium that I knew was both buried and lying about on the surface of the Range. I thought about all the health issues and I realised that the British and Australian governments totally disregarded the safety of the ordinary men working in the forward areas. (Of course their precious boffins were treated differently.) People had, by that time, been suffering and dying for years and I asked myself: 'If the Minor Trials were harmless at Taranaki, why did the British wait until the wind was in the right direction?' Answer: 'Because they wanted the plutonium contamination to blow in a certain direction (actually towards the north or north-west)', away from the other minor trials sites.

In 1972, I heard that the Australian government was going to hand back the Maralinga lands to the State. This meant that the Aborigines would be able to go back and live there. So I said to myself: 'They can't do that, the place is totally unfit for human life with all that contamination.' So I went to the deputy leader of the Labor opposition, Lance Barnard [he would become the Defence Minister when they won the election later in the year]. I put it to him in no uncertain terms that the contamination was shocking and gave him some information so that he could ask some questions of Ransley Victor Garland (Vic) the Minister for Supply. This he did on 14 September 1972 [just before the general election that saw Whitlam sweep to power]. Garland replied by saying that anything that was in Maralinga – any contamination – would have been very much depleted and there would be of no real danger now. That was a bit of a blow because I knew this was not the case – plutonium-239 has a half-life of 24,400 years. The minor tests were conducted in 1960 – that is only 12 years of radioactive decay. What they didn't know was that I had been teaching myself as much as I could about nuclear physics and the biological and medical effects of nuclear radiation. I felt I had to learn as much as possible if I was going to argue the toss about it.

It was clear that Garland hadn't the slightest clue about the hazards of radiation and the physics of the nuclear isotopes produced in the atomic bomb tests. I proved to myself that ordinary people don't need to rely on so-called experts – if you are motivated you can learn and understand anything.

I was working really hard at the time, up to 70 hours a week, so I couldn't put too much time into pursuing my study, but I continued learning and campaigning when I could until 1975 – when the Labor government was kicked out of office.

Then I was ready to have an assault on the government and I started to plot my next move. I sought some advice as to what I could and couldn't say as I had signed the *Official Secrets Act* during my time in the RAAF. I decided to spill the beans in December 1976 – 'blow the whistle' on a grand scale.

Avon campaigning

I went on ABC TV on 'This Day Tonight' with Clive Hale on 2 December 1976, live in Adelaide on a Friday night. It was the most important moment in my life. I put myself in the firing line. It was the beginning of a long saga – those five minutes led me on a long road, to this long-drawn-out controversy and my continuing quest for justice. It completely changed my life. I certainly 'put the cat among the pigeons' and from that day on the subject has never died. I have made sure it hasn't. The programme was something of a bombshell because I was inundated with calls. I went back to the media room as soon as the programme was finished and there were already about 30 reporters waiting, including TV, press and radio. I was totally unprepared for all the hype. It was only 8 pm and it took me until midnight to get away! For example, the *Advertiser* wrote a major article the next day, entitled 'Nuclear waste dump in SA: ex-RAAF man'.

The next day it was all over the country. It blew up to be a pretty big story. Unbeknown to me, a parliamentary gallery reporter from Channel 10 in Canberra, by the name of John Gilbert, was deeply interested in Maralinga. He had been unable to contact me because

Lance Barnard had refused to release my name, fearing there might be serious security repercussions, and he had been waiting for me to show my hand! When I finally got home that night, about 1.30 am, John Gilbert rang and said: 'Don't talk to anyone else. I will come and pick you up in the morning and fly you straight to Maralinga and interview you on the spot. I said: 'Please yourself, that sounds all right to me.' We were up at Maralinga about 11 am on the Saturday.

Maralinga was amazing – the place was totally unguarded. Whether we were there legally or not was irrelevant, we couldn't give two hoots, there was nobody there to stop us. We landed and I took him down to where the graveyard of the radioactive material was and showed him the burial ground. John got it on Channel 10 immediately. He had been waiting for years for this opportunity. Later on, John moved to Sydney with 2GB and I used to get on air with him there quite regularly. I am very grateful to him for giving me such a 'good run' to get the story out.

One week after our trip to Maralinga, Jim Killen, the Minister for Defence in the Fraser Government, announced an internal inquiry into reports of dangerous plutonium waste at the site (see the *Advertiser*, 10 December 1976). I spoke to Shadow Minister Tom Uren's personal assistant about the Minor Trials. I told the assistant that I believed the British were in contravention of the international agreement to halt such tests (see the *Advertiser*, 10 December 1976). This was because during the period 1958–1961, there was an international moratorium on nuclear tests between the UK, the USSR and the USA.

The allegations that I had made against the government were that the British had buried deadly plutonium at Maralinga. This had been denied by Jim Killen. We then had our first big breakthrough on 19 February 1977. See the *Advertiser* for that day, which stated: 'Plutonium in Maralinga Dump – Government. The minister assisting the Minister 0for Defence M. McLeay has confirmed that 20 kilograms of plutonium are buried at Maralinga in SA.' This *really* put the cat among the pigeons. The federal government then had to negotiate with the British government, and after a long-drawn-out argument the British government sent out a team to dig it up, encase it, secure it, and fly it back to Britain. It cost millions of dollars.

In the weeks and months after my 'This Day Tonight' interview, I was flooded with phone calls. I would have much preferred if it had been a little less hectic. I had phone calls every day for weeks up until Christmas when it died down for a couple of weeks, but soon it blew up again. It almost never stopped; it was either the radio or the TV that wanted me, or magazines. I was a little bit hesitant to deal with some, and I became selective in the end because I couldn't keep up with it all – I stuck as far as possible to the mainstream media. Unbeknown to me, there was another chap, Ric Johnstone, who was also in the air force, whom I never knew because he was there in 1956. He was also doing the same type of thing but not with so much publicity. He had formed the Australian Nuclear Veterans Association in Sydney, with a group that was at Maralinga with him. I was totally unaware of him. He became aware of me and he made contact with me and we got together. It was a while before much happened, but there was a small association formed here in Adelaide that did some good work. A Miss Jennifer May organised it (her father was a civilian worker at Maralinga, whom she believed died because of his work there). I lent my support to that for quite awhile. But Ric Johnstone put it to me, in the late 1970s, that we should get together and form a national association in all states. In the meantime, a small group had been formed in Queensland. We plugged on and formed a national association and I became the South Australian coordinator and the small SA association that had been formed earlier, folded-up. I wasn't too pleased about that because they had done some pretty good work.

On Friday, 6 October 1978, I again flew up to Maralinga, this time with the *Advertiser* and TV reporters. Four Commonwealth policemen met us and after a bit of an altercation we were allowed to move around the site, and I took the group over to the plutonium burial site (we called it the graveyard) by the side of the airstrip. The TV people filmed me showing the deep holes in the ground at the graveyard where the earth had subsided. All this was reported in the *Advertiser* on 7 October 1978. The article is entitled: 'N-Waste accuser sees dump again', and correctly reported that I had seen 26 lead boxes buried at the dump, and that I was later told by one of the British boffins that they contained plutonium.

The government panicked, as can be seen from the newspaper reports:

1) Adelaide's *News* on 8 October 1978: 'SA Plutonium Peril: Enough to kill a city'. The report stated: 'There were no serious deterrents to the theft of the plutonium although a small band of Commonwealth police patrolled the area ... there was enough plutonium lying isolated to poison large numbers of people in a major city ... Mr Killen is reported to have said that a small determined band of terrorists could remove the plutonium quickly and use it against the population.'

2) *Financial Review* on 5 October 1978: 'Terrorist threat to British atomic waste. Killen warns on plutonium pile. Federal cabinet has been warned that extremely dangerous plutonium waste from British bomb tests at Maralinga in South Australia could be stolen by terrorists.'

Getting rid of the buried plutonium was no victory in the true sense of the word, but it did show that the government had been in denial for about 15 years since the Minor Trials finished. The buried plutonium was bad enough but imagine how deadly it was out on the Range. The really dangerous plutonium contamination was on the surface of the land – it was still being blown about in the wind. By this time no one knew where this plutonium was. It could have been all around the place, small particles blowing about in the wind. However, our little success rocked the government. In fact, it was the first time that we knew that they were vulnerable. We now felt we had them on the run and they knew that we were a force to be reckoned with.

I probably made most of the running, as Ric Johnstone was more interested in the health effects on the veterans – he was a victim in the true sense of the word. I pursued the issue as broadly as I could. I was also interested in the health effects on both the veterans and their families. But at that time I felt that someone had to expose the dangers of residual radiation that was left behind at Maralinga. I tried, at every opportunity, to force them to confront the question of the clean-up. I continued to pursue them and many times I was contacted

Avon speaking out for a just cause

by the press, especially the Adelaide *Advertiser*, and I have to say they did a splendid job. They ran some very good leading articles relating to the bomb tests. To this day they still give me a fair hearing for which I am most grateful. I continued to campaign during the 1976–1979 period on the basis that the plutonium had to be removed. This was supposed to have been achieved with the clean-up pro-gramme that occurred back in 1967, but it wasn't (see Chapter 9).

In the early 1980s, Ric Johnstone and I became the two main spokespeople for the whole Nuclear Veterans Organisation. He and I never let an opportunity go by to get our message out. We attacked the government on all fronts to expose what went on. In the meantime, the government was on the back foot – they were denying everything.

At some stage I heard about Dr Hedley Marston, an Adelaide scientist and a friend of Sir Mark Oliphant. He became something of a hero of mine, and I only wish I could have met him before he died in 1965. He was Chief of the Division of Biochemistry and General Nutrition in Adelaide, and the one Australian who caught-out the British boffins and our Australian Safety Committee. He did research into radioactive iodine, one of the radioactive substances produced when the atomic bomb explodes. He used this radioactive substance to map where the fallout went by measuring the amount of radioactive iodine in the thyroids of sheep and cattle around Australia (radioactive iodine accumulates in the thyroids of animals, sheep, cattle and human beings). Marston also found that the radioactive cloud from the third bomb test in 1956 drifted over Adelaide. He became alarmed about the biological effects of the radiation entering the food chain, especially radioactive strontium, a very dangerous substance emanating from the bombs. Many years later, his scientific article was rediscovered by the *Advertiser*, and it caused quite a stir.

I followed it up a bit more. Fallout went right across Australia in varying amounts. The concentrations were much higher than was ever admitted at the time. But Marston knew better – he did the tests, he did the research. People like Sir Leslie Martin and Professor Ernest Titterton on the Safety Committee could get whatever they wanted published in the press during the bomb tests, but Marston's work was shunned for many years. There was, I feel, blatant control of the media at the time of the bomb tests. It was one of the most shocking examples of how power is used to suppress the truth.

I have remained actively involved all these years because I am concerned about the way that safety regulations were ignored. All this time there has been a total lack of recognition of the hazards that many thousands of service men and civilians were exposed to during the atomic bomb tests, the Minor Trials, and the clean-ups. The same applies to the damage to the traditional owners of Maralinga, other Aboriginal people and pastoralists who lived in high-risk areas in-line with the radioactive clouds. In many ways my determination to struggle for justice has been spurred-on by the lying and the completely inhumane neglect of all the people who were exposed to radiation.

I pressed for a public inquiry, but the Fraser Government (1978–1983) was in complete denial. They said we could not have an inquiry into things that never happened! Gradually, more and more nuclear veterans came forward, there was a ground swell of support and by about 1980 we had a large number of veterans around the country and more and more were coming forward. At first I couldn't get any of them to speak out – they were all too frightened of breaking the *Official Secrets Act*. I kept telling them: 'Look, I am the bloody proof it's okay, I haven't been put in jail. I haven't been arrested.' It was quite some time before I got people to back me up but gradually some started to speak out. Once the 'genie' was out of the bottle, they couldn't lock all of us up so the game was up; we began to expose the whole rotten core of what went on. During all this time (from 1976 onwards) I had been amassing a huge amount of information, which was sent to me by many different people, some even anonymously. I used to receive big brown envelopes with secret documents in them. I used them to back my public statements to the media, building a damning indictment against the government. I got other documents from 'legal' sources, which I used to good effect.

The information that I received was dynamite. Unfortunately, when I showed it to reporters they were often hesitant to publish anything. They were afraid of the consequences. At least it built my credibility – I wasn't crazy, and I wasn't full of 'bullshit'. Some people had tried to discredit me, saying it was all fiction.

In 1980, I went back to Maralinga again and saw that some of the soil around the pits at the Taranaki site had blown away, exposing some of the debris dumped in them. While there I participated in the making of the film 'Backs to the Blast', which was released in 1981.

Around this time I wanted to get more information into Parliament. I approached Tom Uren to see what he could do. I also met John Scott, Member for Hindmarsh, and I recognised straight away that here was a bloke I could trust. He was fair dinkum. So I told him everything that I felt he could use. He went into Parliament and put his neck on the line and gave them 'bloody hell'. I must say he wasn't afraid to ask questions and dig deep into the whole subject. He was doing this while in opposition as a backbencher. I dealt with him off and on for quite a while – he was first class. He was the only politician that I have met who was also a pretty straight bloke. In 1983, the

Labor government came to power and he pushed for a Royal Commission into the whole sorry mess – he did more than anyone else and I take my hat off to him. I want to put it on the record that the nuclear veterans and the whole of Australia owe him a debt of gratitude.

During all these years, from 1976 to the present day, every time I have appeared on TV or radio, I have received phone calls and letters from people, mostly widows of veterans who had died or who were very sick. Also, children of veterans contacted me wanting help, asking me for advice. All I could do was talk with them and listen to their stories. I heard the most terrible things that happened to their fathers or husbands. The thing that came through most often was that the husbands died young, just when their children really needed them. The wives and children were left alone; the children were brought up without fathers on a widow's pension. It was a miserable existence for them.

I knew bloody well that I couldn't help them. All I could do was offer them advice and moral support. We had no funds or resources – we never got funded by anybody. We couldn't help materially, but we worked to change the government's opinion of their plight. That's how we tried to help people, but most of them just gave up, or died or became despondent.

The government continued to say there had been no danger and no one had died from the effects of radiation. No one had even been affected by radiation. How could one have faith in politicians after that? It is no wonder people have told me that they had a hatred of their own government! I couldn't disagree with them because it was pretty much how I felt. It was a powerless demoralising state of affairs for Ric Johnstone and me. We heard all this for years. We would have liked to help but it wasn't possible.

Eventually, the Royal Commission into the British Nuclear Tests in Australia was established in 1984 – a moment to celebrate. I thought now we will see the truth being told. Justice James McClelland was appointed to lead the Commission – he was a good bloke. I thought everything would come out okay and we would probably be set from there on. Actually, the dead opposite occurred. The Royal

Commission achieved nothing for the veterans. They helped the Aborigines a little, which I am glad for, but the recommendations were worthless to us because the charter of the Royal Commission did not allow it to look into various aspects that would help us. The Commission couldn't help by determining individual cases of exposure to radiation. At the beginning we were naive and we were unaware of that. The Labor government never acted upon even the simple recommendations – like one that there should be a national register of all nuclear veterans. It took another 15 years before a full list of names was published. We lost faith and were extremely disappointed, the system was flawed and it failed us. It is only when you become a victim of the system that you lose faith. I have had no faith in it for a long, long time. It is very unusual if it works for the ordinary person. I believe that in Australia you can still have justice, trouble is you have to buy it! The hard fact underlying our plight is we were not in a war zone when we were posted to Monte Bello, Emu Field, or Maralinga. We were only preparing for war. As armed forces personnel, we obeyed orders to the letter and we did precisely what we were told and many of us subsequently paid the supreme sacrifice – death from radiation-induced diseases. But up to now, all governments have said we cannot receive any compensation or benefits, such as the Gold Card, because we weren't in a war zone. The fact is, we were not up against an enemy that was firing at us. We were up against an invisible enemy which you could not smell, feel or see. Worse than that, we were not told – no one was warned to be cautious. So the invisible enemy may have claimed thousands. Imagine, if there had been a war we would have been heroes. Instead, we are still fighting a bitter struggle against successive governments that have denied there was any danger.

As I have said, many of the veterans just gave up trying after the release of the Report of the Royal Commission. We finally knew that neither the Liberal nor the Labor government had a heart. We were to be wiped from the memory of the country. So it went quiet and things went along for the rest of the 1980s. Occasionally, I would pop my head over the wall and make statements to the press when they contacted me. I lost heart.

The Valiant used to drop an atomic bomb (photographed at Darwin by Avon Hudson)

In the late 1990s there was a revival of interest in Maralinga with the clean-up [see Chapter 10]. I put in my two pennies' worth – mainly dissatisfaction with the corners they were cutting with the clean-up. It played into my hands. I thought, once again, I have got something to say here. It gave me some more opportunities for publicity for the nuclear veterans' plight, and at the same time I got on the bandwagon and tried to influence the course of the clean-up, to no effect.

I hate everything nuclear and I have campaigned against the proposed nuclear waste dump being set up here in South Australia. As I am a member of our local regional council, I have managed to get support from forward-thinking fellow council members and we have made our council area nuclear free.

I met Roger Cross at the Hiroshima Day commemoration in 2001, where we were both speakers. I had already read his book *Fallout: Hedley Marston and the British Bomb Tests in Australia*. Also, about this time, Colin James of the *Advertiser* wrote some excellent articles. He dug deep, uncovering more and more information and I realised that there were still some secret documents that hadn't been released.

People often ask me: 'What has it been like living with this for the last 40 years?' Well it is a bit like living on death row, waiting for the final sentence. You can picture what radiation can do over a long time. It may manifest itself in some cancer or complaint that will do you in. I often think of what might have been if I had not been to Maralinga – life for my family and me would have been much less difficult.

A final word. When I visited Maralinga in 1976, 1978, and 1980 I was told by the Commonwealth police it was too dangerous to walk over the grounds. Does it not strike you as odd that during the years we were there it was not considered dangerous?

Epilogue

We were innocent – lambs to the slaughter – and have been treated with contempt by Australian governments of both political persuasions trying to sweep their tarnished history under the carpet. We *have* suffered; for many of our friends, life was cruelly taken away or changed forever by an unseen and largely unknown foe – ionising radiation. We were naive and trusting of our government. Now they are waiting for us to die. We can no longer deny the collective responsibility to bring our fellows citizens closure. This has been a journey into the dark side of the politics of power and prestige.

The effects of the fallout from the bomb tests were felt much more widely than many have suspected. We have left you with an unsavoury and deadly legacy from a tragic episode in Australia's history.

Australia's involvement in the British bomb tests has only recently been recorded, with more than 16,000 people registered on the government's Nominal Roll of nuclear veterans. This, however, is no indication of both the physical and mental scars inflicted on the nuclear veterans' wellbeing. It is nonetheless important to lay bare our experiences for all to see. This record will help to bring peace of mind to those who suffer as a result of the tests, and promote the cause of a just and honourable resolution to their health problems.

The stories in *Beyond Belief* explain how we became involved and what happened to us and our families. They illustrate the plight of men affected by what they were not told. While they represent a deep scar on Australia's social history, they are, in many ways, stories of adversity and not a little fear. This is uncomfortable history for many a politician, because it cannot be spoken of in the abstract – families are still suffering. At the time of the tests, the Australian public was deliberately and ruthlessly kept in the dark concerning the real effects of the atomic bomb explosions and the so-called Minor Trials.

Our vision for *Beyond Belief* has been to show that this is a human problem. Much like the attitude of some to the stolen generations, it must be faced or we will never be able to believe in the rhetoric that ours is a caring and compassionate society.

The Atomic Weapons Tests Safety Committee (AWTSC), the Australian government's watchdog committee of scientists, deceived the Australian people in pursuit of their own self-interests. The physicists on the Committee were lacking in knowledge of the harmful biological effects of low levels of ionising radiation. Yet they were pledged to take care of Australians, and some were to receive knighthoods and other honours for their 'sterling' work.

Was democracy denied? What of the British? How did they treat Australian civilians and military personnel? We have not attempted to draw a conclusion to such questions. That is not the point. As Sir Mark Oliphant said: 'the onus of proof that they were harmless lies on the side of those who said there was no danger'. We have simply placed our reminiscences on record and hope that you will be able to relate to the invective and our anger about our treatment. We leave it up to you to judge from these pages.

Avon Hudson

Radiation: Its nature and the hazards

Ronald Price

Ordinary people can make judgements about the safety, or otherwise, of being exposed to ionising radiation. Dr Ronald Price, emeritus scholar, La Trobe University, takes us step-by-step through the most important aspects of the science. Various controlling authorities have manipulated the data about the effects of radiation on human health. Ronald has studied this subject for many years, and admires the work of an American physician and scientist, John Gofman, who tried to dispel the myths and lies perpetuated by the pro-nuclear energy and pro-nuclear weapons people.

————

Radiation: Its nature and the hazards

Radiation Sickness: Its severity varies with the individual and his physical condition, the body areas exposed and the amount, kind and intensity of the exposure. The disease may be so slight that the exposed person scarcely notices it, or it may cause severe symptoms.

The systemic reactions to radiation include a general feeling of malaise, loss of appetite or nausea and vomiting and headache.

ENCYCLOPEDIA AND DICTIONARY OF

MEDICINE AND NURSING, 1972.

[I]t is a violation of the most fundamental human rights to impose risks (deaths) upon individuals without their consent. Human rights should not be sacrificed to the pursuit of 'a healthy economy', affluence, progress, science, or any other goal. The whole 'benefit versus risk' doctrine is a profound violation of human rights.

JOHN GOFMAN (1981, p. 415).

Any scientist who thinks that non-scientists cannot comprehend an everyday matter like degrees of uncertainty is probably either demonstrating what this author regards as unjustified contempt, or the common desire to mystify science so that 'ordinary' people will feel overawed by scientific 'experts', especially those who may labour in the service of special interests.

JOHN GOFMAN (1981, p. 812).

Radioactivity and its measurement

Our knowledge of radioactivity has grown substantially over the past 110 years. Roentgen's discovery of X-rays in 1895 altered the prevailing view of the world as consisting of substances made up of solid atoms (from the Greek *a-tomos*, 'uncuttable'). French scientist Antoine Bequerel (1852–1908) then discovered that a salt of the uranium element would blacken a photographic plate, spontaneously giving off radiation similar to X-rays. His work was taken up by the first internationally famous woman scientist, Marie Curie (1867–1934). Born in Poland, she moved to Paris where she worked with her French husband, Pierre Curie, making a number of important discoveries. She died of leukaemia and her notebooks are still too radioactive to be safely handled.

Until the dangers of radiation were realised, radium was used to make watch and clock dials luminous. The workers put their paint-brushes to their lips to tip them, and suffered terribly as a result. X-rays were used in shoe-shops to help with fitting.

Since then our understanding of the structure of matter and the nature and effects of radiation has evolved. Lead covers are now put over patients at the dentist during X-ray photography, and attention is given to the frequency of examinations.

One of those contributing to this understanding was John Gofman, MD, PhD, Emeritus Professor of Medical Physics at the University of California, Berkeley. Gofman was both a physician and doctor of nuclear physics. While working for the Manhattan Project, which produced the atomic bombs dropped on Japan at the end of World War Two, he developed several of the first methods for isolating plutonium. He went on to be Associate Director of the Lawrence Livermore Laboratory from 1962–1969, and founder of their Biomedical Research Division where, at the request of the Atomic Energy Commission, his programme (1963–1972) evaluated the role of certain radiation and chromosome injury in human cancer causation. His warnings of the dangers of radiation have been ignored by the nuclear establishment. They are neither in the interests of the military, who wish to develop nuclear weapons, nor of those who wish to make use of nuclear power facilities. But his books, *Radiation and Human Health* (1981) and *Radiation-induced Cancer: From low-dose exposure* (1990), have been written to allow interested readers to follow his argument and evaluate his conclusions for themselves.

X-rays and the radiation from uranium, called gamma-rays, are classed with the spectrum of radiation which includes ultra-violet, visible light, infra-red, microwaves and radio waves. Originally conceived as wave-like, these are now all considered to consist of minute packets of energy called photons. The different forms of radiation vary in the energy per photon, being smallest for radio waves and highest for X-rays and gamma-rays.

X-rays and gamma-rays differ from the other forms of radiation mentioned in an important way. Because of their high energy per photon they are able to affect both living and non-living materials. To understand this, one must remember that all matter consists of atoms which have a central core (the nucleus) and around this, one or more orbiting electrons, depending on the element. The number of electrons ranges from one for hydrogen through to 92 for uranium. X-rays and gamma-rays are able to knock one of these electrons out of its orbit and give it a very high velocity. This process is called ionisation. The electrically charged atoms that remain are called ions. Furthermore, atoms are combined into molecules, the basic units of such substances as proteins, fats, carbohydrates and the myriad other substances which make up living matter. When ionisation occurs in one or more atoms in one of these substances, considerable disruption is caused, along with all the negative effects of such radiation, whether cancer production or genetic injury.

Two other forms of ionising radiation exist, which are not made up of photons, but particles. One of these is beta-radiation, made up of tiny particles called electrons. The second, alpha-radiation, consists of much larger particles – the nucleus of the element helium, stripped of its two orbiting electrons. Both of these particles, depending on how much energy they possess, cause ionisations when interacting with other matter.

Finally, the non-specialist reading about radiation is confronted with a bewildering number of units, names like curies, becquerels and acronyms like LETs, usually with no attempt to explain them. Some writers even seem to want to mislead their readers, giving numbers which purport to show how safe radiation is. Again, Gofman is the best starting point. His section on 'The Nature of Radioactive Decay and its Measurement' was designed to help the non-scientist. He points out that for purposes of human health, we need to know the quantity of energy being delivered from the radioactive source. This in turn depends on the rate of decay-events and on the amount of energy released per event.

The standard rate of disintegration (decay) was first set as the number of disintegrations per second from one gram of pure radium-226. It was named the curie, after Marie Curie. Since the ability to purify substances, and to measure disintegrations, has improved over time, this number has changed. So the curie has been redefined as the quantity of any radioactive substance which is disintegrating at a rate of 37 billion disintegrations per second. In practice, fractions of this unit are used in physics, chemistry and medicine.

Other common units which need to be understood, are the rad, gray and rem. The first two measure the amount of energy received by a particular quantity of tissue. Thus the rad is one hundred ergs of energy deposited in one gram of tissue, and the gray is one joule of energy deposited in one kilogram of tissue. The erg and joule are simply different ways scientists use to measure the quantity of energy (one joule is equal to ten million ergs). Sometimes the rate of delivery (rads per minute) is medically important, and sometimes the total quantity, irrespective of rate.

The ability of different kinds of radiation to cause ionisations in tissue is a complex question. It depends not only on the quantity of energy carried by the radiation, but also on its speed. Surprisingly, the slower it is, the greater its chance of causing ionisations. In order to describe this situation, the term Linear Energy Transfer (LET) was introduced. This is the amount of energy transferred per unit of path travelled.

The last unit we need to note is the rem. This takes into account the fact that different types of radiation have different abilities to cause ionisation. They are said to have different Relative Biological Effectiveness (RBE). The rem is then the multiple of the rads received and the RBE.

To close this account of measurement and units, one should note that the common instrument used to measure radiation, the Geiger counter, in most cases will not detect alpha particles, and therefore plutonium.

The medical effects of radiation

Many of those who survived the atomic bombing of Hiroshima at the end of World War Two suffered from nausea, vomiting, excessive thirst, loss of appetite, fever, diarrhoea and general malaise. Many sufferered loss of body hair, including the roots. Long-term effects experienced by both Hiroshima and Nagasaki victims include solid cancers, leukaemia, effects on the immune system and genetic damage to their children. While the effect on the immune system caused infections, including tuberculosis, in the first few months, the system returned to normal later.

Australian and British service personnel that were exposed to the tests in Australia in the 1950s reported ill effects, not only in themselves, but also in their children and grandchildren. Immediately, many suffered from rashes, gastro-intestinal ailments, burning eyes and hair loss, conditions similar to those who survived in Japan.

In 1999, Sue Rabbit Roff of Dundee University, published a study she had carried out for the British Nuclear Tests Veterans Associations of Britain and New Zealand, on soldiers who had participated in the tests. Her results would also apply to Australian veterans (Roff, 2003). She reports dental problems, early hair loss, vision problems, hearing loss and tinnitus, various muscularskeletal conditions, skin conditions immediately following exposure, gastro-intestinal conditions, respiratory conditions (asthma), and heart conditions. One third of the cancer deaths in her sample occurred after the cut-off date of a study by the National Radiological Protection Board, which concluded the soldiers' deaths had been no different from those in the general population. Ms Roff notes that slightly less than two thirds of deaths in this sample occurred before the age of 60 years and that one third were caused by cancer.

Ms Roff also reported that many of the veterans suffered from impaired fertility and produced children and grandchildren suffering with birth defects.

None of these conditions are in themselves specific to victims of nuclear radiation. It has therefore been possible for authorities to ignore or deny them. For rigorous scientific proof of causation, careful comparison of chosen groups must be made. Establishments anxious to promote nuclear energy for war or peace have been unwilling to conduct the required studies. Therefore, to gain an understanding of the issue, we must rely on the few who are both qualified and willing to speak out.

Before leaving the topic of the medical effects of radiation, there are one or two other points to be considered. One of these is where the affected person is, in relation to the source, and whether the radiation is external or internal. In the vicinity of atomic explosions, radiation may occur over the whole body if unprotected. It may also occur internally, both in the vicinity of explosions and at great distances from them when fallout is spread through being ingested. When this last occurs, particles with little range of penetration, like alpha particles, can have considerable effect. Particles of different radioactive substances spread in the atmosphere and are deposited in rain and snow. Reports of the British tests speak of the dust falling on uncovered water tanks and exposed field kitchens, thus threatening ingestion of radioactive sources.

The chemical nature of the substance is particularly important, as well as where it goes in the human body. Radioactive iodine, when taken in with the food, passes via the blood to the thyroid where it may interfere with the production of hormones. Rosalie Bertell (1985) notes the release of small quantities of radioactive iodine in the USA from nuclear power plants and large quantities from nuclear reprocessing plants, and regrets that no studies have been made to see if there is a link between this pollution and the over-weight problem.

Other radioactive materials may lodge in the throat and lungs, or in the digestive tract, causing different health problems. Strontium and plutonium are both attracted to the bones, the latter clumping on the surface of them where it irradiates the surrounding tissues with the short-penetrating alpha particles. Strontium, which lodges within the bones, gives off beta particles.

To fully understand the dangers of radioactive substances within the body, it is necessary to understand two other properties. One of these is the physical half-life of the substance. This is the time taken for half the quantity of the substance to give off its radiation and change into another chemical substance. This second substance may or may not itself be radioactive. The other property is the biological half-life. This is the time taken to get rid of half the quantity of the substance by breathing it out, or getting rid of it in the urine or faeces. The danger of a substance obviously depends on the relation between these two measures.

An example of half-lives may make the situation easier to understand. Bertell gives the examples of caesium-137 and strontium-90, both of which have physical half-lives of about 30 years. Caesium-137 is normally got rid of by the body in about two years, while strontium-90 may become part of the bones and remain there throughout the rest of a person's life.

Gofman describes the effect of the introduction of plutonium-238 (half-life 86 years) and plutonium-239 (half-life 24,400 years) into the body. Both of them will be carried in the blood to the liver and the bones. There they will both give off alpha particles. If the same number of atoms are present then the one with the shorter half-life will do more damage. But if quantities with the same number of disintegrations per second are present then the one with the longer half-life will do more damage.

Fallout

When a nuclear explosion occurs, radioactive materials are shot out in all directions. Large quantities are carried into the atmosphere by the heat of the blast, to be deposited later by wind and rain as fallout. Dalton gives a table (taken from Rotblat) of the important fission products in the fallout from nuclear explosions:

Radionuclide	Physical half-life
Iodine-131	8 days
Barium-140	13 days
Ruthenium-103	39 days
Strontium-89	51 days
Yttrium-91	59 days
Zirconium-95	64 days
Cerium-144	284 days

Ruthenium-106	367 days
Caesium-134	2 years
Promethium-147	3 years
Strontium-90	29 years
Caesium-137	30 years
Samarium-151	90 years
Technetium-99	210,000 years
Zirconium-93	1,500,000 years
Caesium-135	3,000,000 years
Iodine-129	16,000,000 years

This table, while giving the half-life of substances, does not show the kind of radiation given off, the substances which each of these elements changes into before reaching a stable (non-radioactive) form, nor the parts of the body where the substance might be lodged to do its damage.

Gofman (1981), in an important chapter on 'Man-made Alpha-particle-emitting Nuclides', discusses the radioactive elements formed in certain nuclear reactors. Some of these are listed in the report on Radiological Safety and Future Land Use at the Maralinga Atomic Weapons Test Range, issued by the Australian Ionising Radiation Advisory Council [AIRAC] in January 1979. They are four forms of plutonium (-238, -239, -240 and -241), and americium-241. The AIRAC's attitude is shown by their comments on this data: that amounts of plutonium and americium present are 'insignificant' and 'it is not conceivable that the amounts [of uranium] possibly deposited would have any significance with respect to human health or ecological well-being.' Of course, they are writing 20 years after the tests, but the half-lives of the elements they list and Gofman's arguments made these statements questionable.

Australians exposed during tests

Twelve atomic bombs were exploded in Australia, seven at Maralinga, two at Emu and three at Monte Bello. Those at Maralinga had epicentres containing an area of seven by four kilometres, which provided overlapping contamination sources at all workplace locations except for the first detonation.

Little or no instruction was given to army personnel on the nature of atomic weapons before taking part in the tests. Major Alan Batchelor, MBE (retired) prepared a report called 'The Nuclear Veteran and the Hazards of Ionising Radiation, 26 March 2002', for the Prime Minister and the Committee for Review of Veterans' Entitlement. In this report he points out that they should have been told of the necessity of protective clothing, the symptoms of radiation sickness, and even the significance of meteorological conditions.

The geology of Maralinga also made conditions particularly dangerous for military personnel working at the test sites. Radioactive materials, mixed with the dust, were easily resuspended during construction activities, and were also moved about by violent dust storms. On at least one occasion, an unexpected change of wind took place, carrying the fallout over camps Roadside and Watson, where there were uncovered water storage tanks and field kitchens in operation.

Where protective clothing was worn, it did not protect against gamma radiation and would only have given a false sense of security. Respirators, when used, were War Department Mark VI light respirators, probably of World War Two vintage. They contained asbestos wool and were not only dangerous on that account, but would have done little to filter the radioactive particles against which they were being worn.

Finally, in Dr John Symonds' book, *A History of British Atomic Tests in Australia*, it is recorded that in tests Hurricane and Totem, Australian aircraft were used for fallout and cloud sampling. These did not carry gamma-ray detection equipment, nor did the aircrew wear protective clothing, film badges or carry dosimeters. No preparations were made for the decontamination of the aircrew or the aircraft.

Safety standards

In the period when the British tested their atomic weapons in Australia, the concern was not so much with safety as with how to conduct atomic war. While the terrible events of Hiroshima and Nagasaki had provided all too much data, the American government, which had control of it, appear to have been in no hurry to release it to others.

Both national and international bodies have pronounced on safety. National bodies include the AIRAC and the American National Council of Radiation Protection (NCRP). The Radiation Effects Research Foundation (RERF), which after 1975 has had control of the Japanese survivor data, is jointly funded by the American and Japanese governments. International bodies include the United Nations Scientific Committee on Effects of Atomic Radiation (UNSCEAR), the Advisory Committee on the Biological Effects of Ionising Radiation (BEIR) and the International Commission on Radiological Protection (ICRP). I will examine the UNSCEAR and BEIR standards below. First let us look at some statements made by the AIRAC in their report on 'operational safety measures and of possible after-effects' in January 1983.

Under 'the underlying premises of radiation protection' (Chapter 6) they compare the concept of risk in occupations involving nuclear radiation with that in other industries and conclude:

> No human activity is wholly free from risk and the underlying philosophy of radiation protection, in which no exposure to radiation is claimed to be 'safe' in an absolute sense, does not differ from that of other occupations.

In the summary and conclusion (Chapter 1) they say:

> The measures taken to protect the public, and the personnel involved in the nuclear test programmes, from radiation injury attributable to the tests were well-planned and almost certainly were effective. The

possibility of incidents, e.g. unauthorised entry to a contaminated area, that may have led to serious unrecorded exposure cannot be completely excluded, but no evidence has been found that any such incident occurred.

Examination of the arguments put forward by Gofman throws grave doubt on the claim that the risk 'does not differ from that of other occupations', while the actual experience of a large number of the Australians who took part in the tests belie the claims of [the above] paragraph.

The BEIR and UNSCEAR analyses

Gofman compares his estimates of radiation-induced cancer with those of BEIR and UNSCEAR (1981, pp. 314–323). Beginning with the BEIR-III Report (1979, draft report), he criticises their 'shuffling of the data' by substituting results from one age cohort for those of another. He comments:

> In a lifetime of scientific research, this author has never seen a more shocking mishandling of scientific evidence than is manifested [by this device] ... Handling data that way, one can 'prove' just about anything one would like to prove (p. 315).

Gofman demonstrates that BEIR also uses wrong percentage figures for the excess cancers per rad:

> On the bases of the analyses in this book and over ten years of writing about and discussing the evidence, this author flatly states that no evidence suggests the correctness of such extremely low percentages per rad as those presented (but not supported) by BEIR-III (p. 317).

He then goes on to show how to obtain the correct percentage excess.

Turning to the UNSCEAR analysis, Gofman shows there are three major flaws in it. They neglect the different effect of age, 'lumping the date for all ages together to arrive at a value corresponding to a whole-body cancer dose'. They base their analysis of the Japanese data on what Gofman shows to be a wrong estimate of absorbed dose. And they do not deal with the problem of a limited duration of follow-up. 'For all these reasons', Gofman concludes, 'the UNSCEAR analysis can hardly be taken as a serious effort to assess the true risk of cancer from population exposure' (p. 323).

There is no safe dose

The support for using nuclear radiation, either as weapons or for generating power and other peaceful purposes, has been that there is some low dose, or dose rate, which is safe. Gofman (1990) refutes this claim:

> With respect to ionising radiation, the meaning of a SAFE dose or dose-rate is a dose or dose-rate at which all exposed persons are safe as the exposure occurs, and all are safe afterwards. NO fraction will be killed later by radiation-induced cancer. In sharp contrast, 'no safe dose or dose-rate' means that no one is safe as the exposure occurs, and afterwards, some FRACTION of the exposed persons will die from radiation-induced cancer, and the rest will be safe from it (Chapter 18–1).

Gofman bases his conclusion that there is no safe dose on both human evidence and logic. The former includes the data from the victims of the atomic bombing of Hiroshima and Nagasaki (Gofman 1981, Chapter 11). In 1990 he added a detailed examination of nine other studies which he considered relevant. But he also examined a number of other studies, showing why he considered them to be irrelevant to settling the issue (Chapter 18). This 'Cancer Difference Method' compared two groups of people who were alike in their cancer risk, but who differed in the radiation dose they received, and asked whether their death rates from cancer were truly different (Chapter 13–1).

Gofman's argument from logic is called Nuclear Track Analysis. Here it is sufficient to note his summation:

Single, primary ionisation-tracks [of fast electrons], acting independently from each other, are never innocuous with respect to creating carcinogenic injuries in the cells which they traverse. Every trace – without help from any other track – has a chance of inducing cancer by creating such injuries (Chapter 18.2).

In the same chapter he goes on to discuss the possible repair of such injuries and emphasises that clinical cancers may require additional conditions to the injury caused by such a single track.

Gofman's conclusion from these analyses was that the cancer-risk per rem of exposure is more severe at low doses than at high doses. This relation is called a supra-linear effect and is worse than the linear relation which is often assumed. Gofman claims that the findings are 'extremely solid' because the data has not been distorted by subdivision or other manipulation (Chapter 13–7).

Gofman's warnings about the danger of low doses of radiation have been supported by a number of reports published since 1990. These are cited in an important article by Dr Rosalie Bertell (Gulf War Syndrome, Depleted Uranium and the Dangers of Low-Level Radiation) available on the Internet (http://ccnr.org/ bertell_book.html). She comments:

In the past few years the information available on the health effects of exposure to low levels of radiation has increased. We are no longer dependent on the commercial or military nuclear researchers who since 1950 have claimed that studies of the effects of low-level radiation are impossible to undertake. The new information is unsettling because it proves the critics of the industry to have been correct as to its serious potential to damage living tissue.

There have also been significant new releases of findings from the atomic bomb research in Hiroshima and Nagasaki, the self-acclaimed 'classical research' of radiation health effects.

All this is in sharp contrast to the Report by G M Watson on behalf of AIRAC (June 1977). Watson is sceptical about even a linear relation between dose and effect, commenting:

> the available evidence suggests that linear extrapolation from the effects of high-doses will tend to exaggerate the effects of small doses of [alpha- or gamma-] radiation, or of larger doses given slowly, but may not overestimate the effects of small doses of heavy particle radiation (p. 22).

A second questionable aspect of that report is the author's treatment of 'natural environmental radiation'. His Table 2 on page 7, gives the impression that the natural radiation dose received in Britain and America is very much higher (and therefore more dangerous) than that received from fallout or occupational exposure and consumer uses. No attempt is made to evaluate these figures. Gofman, on the other hand, goes into some detail and shows exactly what effects may be expected from natural and other sources of radiation and how to calculate them. Finally, Dr Watson would seem to prefer to throw in data from other species of animal when it enables him to downplay the risks of radiation to humans.

Conclusion

Beginning with the Gulf War in Iraq in 1991, and again in Bosnia in 1995, soldiers and civilians have had to suffer the conse- quences of new forms of armaments spreading nuclear radiation. These include the protective armour of tanks and other vehicles, parts of missiles and aircraft, and anti-aircraft and anti-personnel artillery. All of these incorporate so called 'depleted' uranium. That is, uranium containing less than its natural content of uranium-235. Depleted uranium is a waste product of the nuclear-bomb programme and of the production of enriched fuel for nuclear reactors, and is therefore cheap. It is very dense and hard, thus giving strength to armour plating. But it also burns spontaneously on impact, creating tiny particles, which can be inhaled. As much as 70 per cent of a depleted-uranium penetrator bomb can be vaporised when it hits an object.

The danger of such weapons extends far beyond an actual war situation. They form another excuse for the continued mining of uranium, and there is already evidence of increased levels of cancer among those who manufacture them. Then, as with all uses of radioactive materials, there is the problem of accidents in their manufacture, transport and storage. To all these military aspects should be added the hazards of the non-military, or 'peaceful' uses of radioactive materials, especially the continued use and proliferation of nuclear power plants around the world. Finally, and far from least, there is the problem of safe nuclear waste disposal, a problem that despite all official reassurances is clearly insoluble.

Those concerned with a future for humankind take heed, the danger is unseen – we have much to learn from Gofman's timely warnings.

———

Ronald has demonstrated how low doses of radiation can be extremely harmful to human health and that extreme precautions ought to be taken to prevent exposure. The British were well aware of the dangers, though their usual defence is that in the 1950s, the world did not know or understand the risks. This is nonsense. The Range Standing Orders for Maralinga, issued by the Health Physics group, clearly demonstrates that this assertion is totally wrong.

Maralinga Range areas were colour coded as follows:

Yellow Areas – Risk of serious contamination
Red Areas – Risk of slight contamination
Blue Areas – No contamination risk, but penetrating radiation present

But Avon Hudson states that for the first months of his work during the Minor Trials period, he was not told what the colours meant. Also, there was a fleet of contaminated vehicles (the so-called 'hot' fleet) that were painted yellow and kept out on the Range. He and other Australians, as well as many British servicemen, drove these vehicles without any protective clothing.

The Standing Orders also state that 'under no circumstances shall anyone eat, drink or smoke in an active area'–this too was not enforced. The Orders also required persons who were leaving a contaminated area to be checked by a Health Physics person–often this did not take place. Another Order that was ignored was that 'the smallest cut sustained while in an active area shall be treated seriously and reported to a Health Physics representative'.

It is clear that the Standing Orders were systematically ignored by the authorities and many veterans were not even aware of the provisions that related to their particular work. It is evident that the authorities had no intention of protecting the military or civilian workforce.

Appendices

1. British atomic weapons tests in Australia

MONTE BELLO ISLANDS – Operation Hurricane
2 Oct 1952   25 kt – fired at 0800 hours

EMU FIELD – Operation Totem
15 Oct 1953   10 kt – fired 0700 hours
27 Oct 1953   8 kt – fired 0700 hours

MONTE BELLO ISLANDS – Operation Mosaic
16 May 1956   15 kt – fired 1150 hours
19 June 1956   60 kt – fired 1014 hours

MARALINGA – Operation Buffalo
Buffalo Series
27 Sept 1956   15 kt – fired 1700 hours
4 Oct 1956   1.5 kt – fired 1630 hours
11 Oct 1956   3 kt – fired 1427 hours
22 Oct 1956   10 kt – fired 0005 hours

MARALINGA – Operation Antler
Antler Series
14 Sept 1957   0.9 kt – fired 1435 hours
25 Sept 1957   5.67 kt – fired 1000 hours
9 Oct 1957   26.6 kt – fired 1615 hours

MARALINGA – Taranki, Minor Trials (1958–1962)
Wewak (VK33, VK60A, VK60C)
Naya (TM100)
Naya (TM101)
Kittens*

*There was a small trial at Emu also called Kittens, Kuli, Dobo

2. The Minor Trials: Radioactive materials used

Location	Trial	Date	Quantity (kg)
	PLUTONIUM		
Taranaki	Vixen B	1960–1963	22.2
Naya 1 (TM100)	Tims	1960	0.6
Naya (TM101)	Tims	1961	0.6
Wewak (VK33)	Vixen A	1959	0.008
Wewak (VK60A)	Vixen A	1961	0.294
Wewak (VK60C)	Vixen A	1961	0.277
	BERYLLIUM		
Emu	Kittens	1953	0.036
Naya	Kittens	1955–1957	0.75
Naya	Tims	1957	1.60
Kuli – TM11	Tims	1959–1960	26.20
Kuli – TM16	Tims	1960–1961	39.00
Kuli – TM5	Tims	1961	10.00
Wewak – VK29	Vixen A	1959	0.140
Wewak – VK28	Vixen A	1959	0.250
Wewak – VK27	Vixen A	1959	0.230
Wewak – VK30	Vixen A	1959	0.100
Wewak – 60A	Vixen A	1961	1.720
Wewak – 60B	Vixen A	1961	1.720
Taranaki	Vixen B	1961–1963	17.60
Total			99.35

Location	Trial	Date	Quantity (kg)
URANIUM (U-235 and U-238) – Depleted Uranium			
			U-238/U-235
Naya 3	Tims	1955	138.0
Kuli – TM4	Tims	1956–1960	6605.0
Kuli – TM11	Tims	1959–1960	67.0
Kuli – TM16	Tims	1960–1963	731.0
Kuli – TM50	Tims	1961	90.0
Kittens Area	Kittens	1955–1957	120.0
Naya 1	Rats	1956–1958	151.0
Naya	Kittens	1957	5.0
Naya 2	Kittens	1960–1962	32.0
Naya 3	Kittens	1957	23.4
Wewak	Vixen A		67.8
Dobo	Rats		28.0
Taranaki	Vixen B		24.9/22.4
Totals			8083/22.4

3. Total number of British tests excluding the minor trials at Maralinga

Country	Total	Atmospheric	Underground
Australia	12	12	0
Malden Island	3	3	0
Christmas Atoll	6	6	0
Nevada (USA)	23	0	23
Total	44	21	23

Taken from *L'héritage de la bombe*, Bruno Barrillot

4. Estimated number of tests by the nuclear-bomb club 16 July 1945–16 May 1998

Country	Total	Atmospheric	Underground
USA	1028	215	813
USSR	715	219	496
France	210	50	160
Britain	44	21	23
China	45	23	22
India	4	0	4
Pakistan	2	0	2
Total	2048	528	1520

Taken from *L'héritage de la bombe*, Bruno Barrillot

Suggested Further Reading

The story of the atomic bomb tests in Australia has been told many times. You can read about them in a number of books devoted to the subject and by consulting the report of The Royal Commission into British Nuclear Tests in Australia, published in 1985. A good starting point for learning more is Robert Milliken's book *No Conceivable Injury*.

Arnold, L. 1987. *A Very Special Relationship: British atomic weapon trials in Australia*. London: Her Majesty's Stationery Office.

Australian Ionising Radiation Advisory Council. 1979. *Radiological Safety and Future Land Use at the Maralinga Atomic Weapons Test Range. Report AIRAC 4*. Canberra: Australian Government Printing Service.

Australian Ionising Radiation Advisory Council and Bureau of Meteorology. 1975. *Fallout Over Australia from Nuclear Tests*. Canberra: Australian Government Publishing Service.

Australian Ionising Radiation Advisory Council. 1983. *British Nuclear Tests in Australia – A review of operational safety measures and of possible after-effects, Report No. 9*. Canberra: Australian Government Publishing Service.

Barrillot, B. 2002. *L'héritage de la Bombe Sahara, Polynésie (1960–2002): Les Faits, les Personnels, les Populations*. Lyon, France: Centre de Documentation et de Recherche sur la Paix et les Conflits.

Barrillot, B. 2003. *Les Irradiés de la République. Les Victimes des Essais Nucléaires Français Prennent la Parole*. Bruxelles: Editions Complexe.

Batchelor, A. 2002. *Veterans and the Hazards of Ionising Radiation*. Report submitted to Committee of Review of Veterans Entitlements.

Beadle, L. 1967. *Blast the Bush*. Adelaide: Rigby.

Beale, H. 1977. *This Inch of Time*. Melbourne: Melbourne University Press.

Bertell, R. 1985. *No Immediate Danger: Prognosis for a radioactive earth*. London: The Women's Press.

Blackeway, D. and Lloyd-Roberts, S. 1985. *Fields of Thunder: Testing Britain's bomb*. Sydney: Unwin.

Blake, J R, Dwyer, L J, Martin, J H and Titterton, E W. 1960. 'Global Fallout During 1959', *Australian Journal of Science*, 3, 23, 69–71.

Blake, J R, Dwyer, L J, Moroney, J R, Stevens, D J and Titterton, E W. 1962. 'Global Fallout in Australia During 1960–1961', *Australian Journal of Science*, 12, 24, 467–470.

Bok, S. 1978. *Lying: Moral choice in public and private life*. New York: Pantheon Books.

Bryant, F J, Dwyer, L J, Martin, J H and Titterton, E W. 1959. 'Strontium-90 in the Australian Environment, 1957–58', *Nature*, 184, 755–760, 4689.

Bryant, F J, Dwyer, L J, Moroney, J R, Stevens, D J and Titterton, E W. 1962. 'Strontium-90 in the Australian Environment 1957 to 1960', *Australian Journal of Science*, 10, 24, 397–409.

Burns, P A, Cooper, M B, Duggleby, J C, Mika, J F and Williams, G A. 1986. *Plutonium-contaminated Fragments at the Taranaki Site at Maralinga*. Yallambie, Victoria: Australian Radiation Laboratory.

Butement, W A S, Dwyer, L J, Eddy, C F, Martin, L H and Titterton, E W. 1957. 'Radioactive Fallout in Australia from Operation "Mosaic"', *Australian Journal of Science*, 125–135, 205.

Butement, W A S, Dwyer, L J, Martin, L H, Stevens, D J and Titterton, E W. 1958. 'Radioactive Fallout in Australia From Operation Buffalo', *Australian Journal of Science*, 3, 21, 63–78.

Camilleri, J. 1984. *The State and Nuclear Power*. Ringwood, Victoria: Penguin.

Caro, D E and Martin, R L. 1987. 'Leslie Harold Martin 1900–1983', *Historical Records of Australian Science*, 1, 17, 97–107.

Cathcart, D B. 1994. *Test of Greatness: Britain's struggle for the atom bomb*. London: JohnMurray.

Cawte, A. 1992. *Atomic Australia*. Kensington: New South Wales University Press.

Christian, J. 1996. 'Cleaning up our Nuclear Past', *Good Weekend*, June 22, 18–24.

Clark, I and Wheeler, N J. 1989. *The British Origins of Nuclear Strategy, 1945–1955*. Oxford: Clarendon Press.

Cockburn, S and Ellyard, D. 1981. *Oliphant: The life and times of Sir Mark Oliphant*. Adelaide: Axiom Books.

Cook, W. 1967. *Operation Brumbie* [sic] *Final Report*. Aldermaston, UK: AWRE.

Cronin, V. 1971. *Napoleon*. London: William Collins.

Cross, R T. 2000. 'Hedley Ralph Marston', *Australian Dictionary of Biography, Vol 15*, (ed. Ritchie, J.), 310–312. Melbourne: Melbourne University Press.

Cross, R T. 2001. *Fallout: Hedley Marston and the British bomb tests in Australia*. Adelaide: Wakefield Press.

Cross, R. T. 2003. 'British Nuclear Tests and the Indigenous People of Australia', in Holdstock, D. and Baranaby, F. (eds), *The British Nuclear Weapons Programme 1952–2002*, 76–90. London: Frank Cass.

Dalton, L. 1991. *Radiation Exposures*. Newham, Victoria: Scribe Publications.

Darby, S C, Kendall, G M, Fell, T P, Doll, R, Goddill, A A, Conquest, A J, Jackson, D A and Haylock, R G E. 1993. *Mortality and Cancer Incidence 1952–1990 in UK Participants in the UK Atmospheric Nuclear Weapon Tests and Experimental Programmes*. Didcot: National Radiological Protection Board and the Imperial Cancer Research Fund.

Department of Veterans' Affairs, 2001. *Preliminary Nominal Roll of Australian Participants in the British Atomic Tests in Australia*. Department of Veterans' Affairs: Woden, ACT.

Dwyer, L J, Keam, D W, Stevens, D J and Titterton, E W. 1957. 'Search for Fallout in Australia from the Christmas Island Tests', *Australian Journal of Science*, 2, 20, 39–41.

Dwyer, L J, Martin, J H, Stevens, D J and Titterton, E W. 1959. 'Radioactive Fallout in Australia from Operation Antler', *Australian Journal of Science*, 3, 22, 97–106.

Glasstone, S and Dolan, P J (eds). 1980. *The Effects of Nuclear War*, Third Edition. UK: Castle House Publications prepared by the United States Department of Defense and the United States Department of Energy.

Gofman, J W. 1981. *Radiation and Human Health*. San Francisco: Sierra Club Books.

Gofman, J W. 1990. *Radiation-induced Cancer from Low-dose Exposure: An independent analysis*. San Francisco: Committee for Nuclear Responsibility Inc.

Gofman, J W. 1995. *Preventing Breast Cancer: The story of a major, proven, preventable cause of this disease*. San Francisco: Committee for Nuclear Responsibility Inc.

Goodfield, J (ed.) 1991. *Weapons in the Wilderness: The exploitation of the north-west of South Australia*. Adelaide: Anti Bases Campaign.

Gowing, M. 1974. *Independence and Deterrence, Vols. 1 and 2*. London: Macmillan.

Grahlfs, F L. 1996. *Voices from Ground Zero: Recollections and feelings of nuclear test veterans*. Lanham: University Press of America.

Hamersley, H and Moroney, J. 1985. *Hedley R. Marston, F.R.S. and the Atomic Weapons Tests Safety Committee – The controversy over fallout from British nuclear tests in Australia in 1956: A chronological overview of the controversy*. Submission to the Royal Commission. Yallambie, Victoria: Australian Radiation Laboratory.

Holdstock, D and Baranaby, F (eds). 2003. *The British Nuclear Weapons Programme 1952–2002*. London: Frank Cass.

Holmes, C H. 1952. 'Half-Way Round the World to Test Atomic Weapons', *Walkabout*, July, 10–15.

International Physicians for the Prevention of Nuclear War (IPPNW). 1991. *Radioactive Heaven and Earth: The health and environmental effects of nuclear weapons testing in, on, and above the earth*. New York: The Apex Press.

Johnston, P N, Burns, P A, Cooper, M B and Williams, G A. 1988. *Isotopic Ratios of Actinides Used in British Nuclear Trials at Maralinga and Emu*. Yallambie, Victoria: Australian Radiation Laboratory.

Keam, D W, Dwyer, L J, Martin, J H, Stevens, D J and Titterton, E W. 1958. 'Global Fallout in Australia During the Period 26 November 1956 to 31 December 1957', *Australian Journal of Science*, 1, 8–9, 21.

Keam, D W, Dwyer, L J, Martin, J H, Stevens, D J and Titterton, E W. 1958. 'Experiments on the "Sticky Paper" Method of Radioactive Fallout Sampling', *Australian Journal of Science*, 4, 21, 99–104.

Keam, D W, Dwyer, L J, Martin, J H and Titterton, E W. 1959. 'Global Fallout in Australia During 1958', *Australian Journal of Science*, 1, 22, 51–54.

Lokan, K H. 1985. *Residual Radioactive Contamination at Maralinga and Emu*. Yallambie, Victoria: Australian Radiation Laboratory.

Love, R (ed.) 1987. *If Atoms Could Talk: Search and serendipity in Australian science*. Richmond, Victoria: Greenhouse.

McClelland, J, Fitch, J and Jones, W J A. 1985. *Royal Commission into British Nuclear Tests in Australia, Vols. 1 and 2*. Canberra: Australian Government Publishing Service.

MacLeod, R. 1994. 'The Atom Comes to Australia: Reflections on the Australian nuclear programme, 1953 and 1993', *History and Technology*, 11, 299–315.

MacLeod, R. 1994. 'Nuclear Knights vs Nuclear Nightmares: Experts as advocates and emissaries in Australian nuclear affairs', in Cabral, R (ed.) Debating the Nuclear-Science, Technology, Ideology, *Culture*, 7, 97–112, Gothenburg: Gothenburg University.

Marsden, E. 1959. 'Radioactivity of Soils, Plant Ashes and Animal Bones', *Nature*, 183, 923–925.

Marston, H R. 1958. 'The Accumulation of Radioactive Iodine in the Thyroids of Grazing Animals Subsequent to Atomic Weapon Tests', *Australian Journal of Biological Sciences*, 11, 382–398.

Martin, B. 1980. *Nuclear Knights*. Dickson: Rupert Public Interest Movement.

Middlesworth Van, L. 1954. 'Radioactivity in Animal Thyroids from Various Areas', *Nucleonics*, 9, 12, 56–57.

Middlesworth Van, L. 1956a. 'Radioactivity in Thyroid Glands Following Nuclear Weapon Tests', *Science*, 123, 982–983, 3205.

Middlesworth Van, L. 1956b. 'Iodine-131 Fallout in Bovine Fetus', *Science*, 128, 597–598, 3324.

Middlesworth Van, L. and Melick, R. 1959. 'Thyroid I131 Content of Victorian Lambs in Relation to Nuclear Weapons Tests', *The Medical Journal of Australia*, May 16, 664–665.

Milliken, R. 1986. *No Conceivable Injury: The story of Britain and Australia's atomic cover-up*. Ringwood, Victoria: Penguin.

National Radiation Advisory Committee. 1958. *Information for the Prime Minister on the Report, August 1958, of the Scientific Committee on the Effects of Atomic Radiation to the Thirteenth General Assembly of the United Nations*. Melbourne: Department of Supply.

Newton, J O. 1992. 'Ernest William Titterton 1916–1990', *Historical Records of Australian Science*, 2, 9, 167–187.

Navias, M S. 1992. *Nuclear Weapons and British Strategic Planning, 1955–1958*. Oxford: Clarendon Press.

Pauling, L. 1958. 1983. *No More War!* New York: Dodd, Mead & Company.

Pearce, N. 1984. *United Kingdom Atomic Energy Authority: Final report on residual radioactive contamination of the Maralinga Range and the Emu site*. AWRE Report No 0-16-68. Aldermaston: AWRE.

Phillpot, H R. 1959. *Meteorology and Atomic Energy: Selected areas of radioactive fallout from nuclear explosions*. Project report 59/2328, Bureau of Meteorology.

Roff Rabbit, S. 2003. 'Long-term Health Effects in UK Test Veterans', in
D. Holdstock and F. Barnaby (eds) *The British Nuclear Weapons
Programme 1952–2002*, 101–114. London: Frank Cass.

Ruthven, K. 1993. *Nuclear Criticism*. Melbourne: Melbourne
University Press.

Sherratt, T. 1985. 'A Political Inconvenience: Australian scientists at the
British atomic weapons tests, 1952–53', *Historical Records of
Australian Science*, 2, 6, 137–152.

Smith, J. 1985. *Clouds of Deceit: The deadly legacy of Britain's bomb
tests*. London: Faber & Faber.

Symonds, J L. 1985. *A History of British Atomic Tests in Australia*.
Canberra: Commonwealth Department of Resources and Energy.

Tame, A and Robotham, F P J. 1982. *Maralinga: British A-bomb
Australian legacy*. Melbourne: Fontana.

The National Radiation Advisory Committee. 1965. *Report to the Prime
Minister by The National Radiation Advisory Committee*. Canberra:
Commonwealth Government Printer.

Titterton, E W. 1956. *Facing the Atomic Future*. Melbourne:
F.W. Cheshire.

Titterton, E W. 1959. 'Radioactivity of Soils, Plant Ashes and Animal
Bones', *Nature*, 183, 924.

Titterton, E W. and Robotham, F.P. 1979. *Uranium Energy Source of
the Future? The case for– E.W. Titterton; the case against– F.P.
Robotham*. West Melbourne: Thomas Nelson ABACUS.

Titterton, E W. 1985. 'Letter to the Editor on "Nuclear Weapon Tests"',
Search, 1–2, 16, February to March.

Wise, K N and Moroney, J R. 1985. 1992. *Public Health Impact of
Fallout from British Nuclear Weapons Tests in Australia,
1952–1957*. Yallambie, Victoria: Australian Radiation Laboratory.

Contributors

Researchers and writers
Patricia Donnelly provided accounts written by civilians. The following people contributed by writing chapters: Ronald Price wrote on the nature of radiation and its effects on human health. Doug Rickard provided Chapter 7 – the story of an Aussie bloke and the element cobalt. Alan Parkinson wrote the account of the latest clean-up of Maralinga (Chapter 10). Bruno Barrillot wrote Chapter 11 (translated from the French by Jennifer MT Carter) showing the plight of people affected by the French tests.

Navy
Douglas Brooks, Bob Dennis, Jerry Lattin and Dick Sundstrom.

Air force
John Bradley, Norman Geschke and Avon Hudson.

Army
Audrey Jones (for William Jones) and Peter Webb.

Commonwealth police
Dorothy Bell (for Edward Bell)

Civilians directly involved in the test sites
Mara Marchioro (for Drago (Joe) Anicic), Joseph Baker, Patricia Donnelly (for Owen and Terry Donnelly), Vera Edwards (for Robert Schmidt), R W Elborough, Pat Finch, Terrance May, Patrick O'Connell, Mike Robinson, Gary Ryan, George Stirna.

Civilians not directly involved in the test sites
Eileen Kampakuta Brown, Dennis Cole, Peter W Harvey, Almerta Lander, Jessie Lennon, Yami Lester, Millie Taylor and Edna and Jessie Williams.

British Servicemen
Sam McGee (RAF)

Scientific and Technical
Edwin Bailey, Ian McKiggan, Alan Parkinson, Brian Potter and Doug Rickard

Abbreviations and Useful Terms

ACS: Australian Construction Services
AERE: Atomic Energy Research Establishment, Harwell, Britain
AHPT: Australian Health Physics Team
AIRAC: Australian Ionising Radiation Advisory Council
ARDU: Australian Radiological Detection Unit
AWRE: British Atomic Energy Research Establishment,
    Aldermaston, Britain
AWTSC: Atomic Weapons Tests Safety Committee
BEIR: Advisory Committee on the Biological Effects of Ionising
    Radiation
ARL: Australian Radiation Laboratory
ARPANSA: Australian Radiation Protection and Nuclear Safety
    Agency
CSIRO: Commonwealth Scientific and Industrial Research
    Organisation
CXRL: Commonwealth X-ray and Radium Laboratories
DPIE: Commonwealth Department of Primary Industries and
    Energy
DVA: Department of Veterans' Affairs, Canberra
ICRP: International Commission on Radiological Protection
IPPNW: International Physicians for the Prevention of Nuclear
    War
MARTAC: Maralinga Rehabilitation Technical Advisory
    Committee

NCRP: National Council of Radiation Protection, America
RDU: Radiation Detection Unit, Department of Defence
RERF: Radiation Effects Research Foundation
TAG: Technical Assessment Group
UNSCEAR: United Nations Scientific Committee on Effects of
    Atomic Radiation
WRE: Weapons Research Establishment, Salisbury, South
    Australia

Useful Terms

Clean Bombs: Smaller than normal amounts of radioactivity
    released.
Dirty Bombs: Larger than normal amounts of radioactivity
    released.
Ground zero: Exact site of an atomic bomb explosion.
Overburden: Clean material (such as soil) used to cover
    contaminated material.
Rainouts: When rain occurs in the presence of a radioactive cloud
    large amounts of radioactivity are deposited.
Yield in kilotons: The equivalent amount of TNT explosive that
    would casue the same explosive capacity. Note it does not
    refer to the amount of radioactivity released.

Acknowledgements

This book could not have been contemplated, let alone written, without the encouragement and participation of all of the contributors and many other well-wishers. A very special thanks goes to the contributors, who rightly own this book. The task of selecting the contributors' accounts was often a painful one for us. At least three of our contributors died very soon after providing their reminiscences. You will find the list of contributors elsewhere in the book. Suffice to say here that we were not able to include all the contributions we received, nor were we able to include everything that was written by the selected contributors. We have tried to keep to our intent of letting the accounts tell the actual history.

We thank Ian McKiggan, investigative journalist, who collected stories from men who witnessed, or who were in some way involved. We especially thank him for Dennis Cole's story, (see Chapter 2).

Some of our contributors and supporters have been researchers and writers in support of the book, and they have written separate chapters of the book. We especially thank Alan Parkinson, Ronald Price and the now deceased Doug Rickard for their contributions. *Beyond Belief* is a collective effort and as painful as some of the experiences have been for some of the contributors to tell they have done so in order that we may all learn for the past, and record a few of the human events that occurred – we thank them all.

We owe a deep debt of gratitude to Patricia Donnelly, without her efforts we would not have obtained the stories of the civilians. She is an expert in locating people and convincing them to put pen to paper to record their personal histories. She, single-handedly, supplied all of the stories written by the civilians. To Mike Robinson and Michele Madigan for their help with the experiences of the Aboriginal people.

We acknowledge and thank Colin James of the *Advertiser* in Adelaide. His encouragement and the inspiration that we initially gained from his series of articles written in that newspaper in 2001, and later for his personal encouragement, have been much appreciated. His articles were a model of investigative journalism for a social purpose and did much to advance the cause of the atomic bomb servicemen, Aboriginal people, pastoralists, civilian workers and families of all who had contact with the British atomic bomb tests. They did much to inspire us to make a collection of stories from which this book emerged. Peter Butt, film maker of Silent storm whose efforts at bringing to a wide TV audience the story of deadly strontium-90 encouraged us along the way. We thank Mike Sexton, ABC journalist, for providing material to add to Sam McGee's story and for his support. Thanks are due to Mrs Trish van Dyk who wrote about Almerta Lander's experiences with the Black Mist Incident (Almerta's eyes being very poor), see Chapter 3, and thanks to Almerta for her important story. She has a wonderfully clear memory.

Bruno Barrillot (Centre de Documentation et de Recherche sur la Paix et les Conflits, 187 montée de Choulans, F–69005 Lyon, France) kindly wrote a brief description of the efforts of the French nuclear veterans, which was translated by Jenny Carter.

We thank Ron (now deceased) and Irene Gray for their assistance in tracking down some of the people affected by the bomb tests. It was the Grays and Dennis Matthews, a prominent anti-nuclear activist and environmentalist in Adelaide, who were the driving force behind the 2001 Hiroshima Day commemorations that finally brought Cross and Hudson together.

One of us (Roger Cross) thanks the Department of Science

and Mathematics Education, University of Melbourne, for support during 2002 in providing him with research time away from the University and the members of the staff for their encouragement. Roger also thanks the media personalities who gave him such a fair hearing on the publication of his last book, *Fallout*. They include, in addition to Colin James, Phillip Adams of ABC Radio National and The *Australian*; and Norrie Ross, and Nick Richardson, of Melbourne's *Herald Sun*. Their support brought him into closer contact with both civilian veterans and ex-servicemen and led directly to the collaboration that has resulted in this book.

Avon Hudson, acknowledges all the people who have supported him during his thirty-year campaign for recognition and a fair resolution to the issues of compensation. He wishes to place on record the tremendously important role of some of the Australian media – a perhaps surprising assertion in an era where the media has often been accused of lying in bed with those who would cover-up difficult and confronting issues of our time. Avon acknowledges the support and help of the *Advertiser* newspaper and journalists such as David English, Peter De Ionno, Bob Whitington and latterly Colin James. He also acknowledges Clive Hale compare of 'This Day Tonight', ABC TV and John Gilbert ex-Canberra Press Gallery and Channel 10 for encouragement. He thanks two politicians who actually listened and tried to help: Tom Uren (formally Member for Reid) and John Scott (formally Member for Hindmarsh). Finally, he acknowledges the wonderful work done by D R 'Ric' Johnstone, Australian Nuclear Veterans' Association (incorporated in NSW) for the work done over many years for the nuclear veterans.

We acknowledge the work of Senator Lyn Allison, Australian Democrats, for the way she has relentlessly pursued the government over the issues surrounding the bomb tests. We were encouraged along the way by many people and while we cannot mention them all, single out Dr John Carter and filmmaker, Peter Butt, for their support and belief in this project.

We record our grateful thanks to the staff of Wakefield Press, an independent long-established Australian publisher, and in particular to Michael Bollen for his belief in the book and his wise counsel, and to Ryan Paine for his superb editing skills. Without the increasingly rare independence in the Australian publishing scene, this book may never have seen the light of day.

We are indebted to many people who went out of their way to assist us; they are too numerous to mention here, we thank them all.

Finally, we thank our wives, Jenny Carter and Annette Hudson for helping to bring this project to a conclusion. Annette has supported Avon's 30-year campaign for justice, and Jenny provided inspiration, the translation of Bruno Barrillot's contribution, advice and editing skills.

Roger Cross
Avon Hudson

Also by Wakefield Press

Fallout

Hedley Marston and the British bomb tests in Australia

Roger Cross

Fallout is the strange but true story of a celebrated Australian scientist's involvement in the 1956 British atomic bomb tests. Hedley Marston, an idol with his own feet of clay, was determined not only to reveal official lies and chicanery, but to expose as charlatans the Australian scientists who were appointed to protect the nation from any possible harm. Contrary to official pronouncements, radioactive fallout was blowing across the country and contaminating many towns and communities, including Marston's beloved Adelaide. The dispute that ensued was perhaps the most acrimonious in the history of Australian science.

Fallout tells us much about the nature of science and our society. It is about science in service of the bomb, and in service of self. Roger Cross tells a story that must make us ask the alarming question: could we be fooled again?

'A very readable story.' – David Day, *Age*

For more information visit www.wakefieldpress.com.au

Also by Wakefield Press

Chance and Commitment

Memoirs of a medical scientist

Basil S. Hetzel AC, MD

Some discoveries have changed forever the fight against disease or the treatment of a medical condition: penicillin, a vaccine against polio, the bionic ear, and . . . iodized salt.

Dr Basil Hetzel's work as a research scientist and public health advocate has prevented millions worldwide from being born intellectually disabled. Hetzel and his team discovered in the 1960s that a single dose of iodized oil given to pregnant women could forestall many potential birth defects. Later he began his crusade to persuade the governments of Indonesia, Nepal, Tibet, India, the People's Republic of China and many other affected countries to add iodine to salt in order to eliminate this centuries old 'scourge of mankind'.

Chance and Commitment: Memoirs of a Medical Scientist traces the life and work behind Dr Hetzel's iodine crusade and his many other endeavours in the cause of public health. It tells the story of a medical student who wanted no more than to be a good physician like his father and became a renowned research scientist. Basil Hetzel has travelled from Adelaide to the Great Hall of the People in Beijing, from working at the laboratory bench to being named a Living National Treasure.

For more information visit www.wakefieldpress.com.au

Also by Wakefield Press

Beautiful Lies

Australia from Menzies to Howard

Tony Griffiths

Beautiful Lies is an original account of the people, events and forces that have shaped Australia since the Second World War. It is racy, maverick and impartial – a tour de force.

Tony Griffiths is an author and historian who has taught Australian and Scandinavian history for a quarter of a century at universities in Australia, Scandinavia and Europe.

'Tony Griffiths makes Australian history seem effortless, in the very best sense of the word. He manages to cover the events of more than half a century at a rollicking pace, while capturing all the important details – and a vast number of amusing ones – along the way. His talent for language yields gems.' – Jo Case, Australian Bookseller and Publisher

For more information visit www.wakefieldpress.com.au

Wakefield Press is an independent publishing and
distribution company based in Adelaide, South Australia.
We love good stories and publish beautiful books.
To see our full range of titles, please visit our website at
www.wakefieldpress.com.au.

 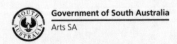

Wakefield Press thanks Fox Creek Wines
and Arts South Australia for their support.